Jacquelyn Kay Thompson

Caring on the Streets: A Study of Detached Youthworkers

Caring on the Streets: A Study of Detached Youthworkers has been co-published simultaneously as *Child & Youth Services*, Volume 19, Number 2 1999.

More pre-publication
REVIEWS, COMMENTARIES, EVALUATIONS . . .

"**T**he discussion of the content
and outcomes of detached
youthwork is interesting and in-
formative. . . . The last two chapters constitute the wings by which
her book soars through the ether
of paradox, ambiguity, confusion,
and calling. . . . The comments on
supervision are themselves worth
the price of admission and ought
to be required reading by every
supervisor in America."

Bruce R. Thomas, BA
Executive Director
Youthworks
Chicago, Illinois

The Haworth Press, Inc.

Caring on the Streets:
A Study
of Detached Youthworkers

Caring on the Streets: A Study of Detached Youthworkers has been co-published simultaneously as *Child & Youth Services*, Volume 19, Number 2 1999.

The *Child & Youth Services*™ Monographic "Separates"

Series Editor: Jerome Beker, Professor, Youth Studies Program, School of Social Work, University of Minnesota

Below is a list of "separates," which in serials librarianship means a special issue simultaneously published as a special journal issue or double-issue and as a "separate" hardbound monograph. (This is a format which we also call a "DocuSerial")

"Separates" are published because specialized libraries or professionals may wish to purchase a specific thematic issue by itself in a format which can be separately cataloged and shelved, as opposed to purchasing the journal on an on-going basis. Faculty members may also more easily consider a "separate" for classroom adoption.

"Separates" are carefully classified separately with the major book jobbers so that the journal tie-in can be noted on new book order slips to avoid duplicate purchasing.

You may wish to visit Haworth's website at . . .

http://www.haworthpressinc.com

. . . to search our online catalog for complete tables of contents of these separates and related publications.

You may also call 1-800-HAWORTH (outside US/Canada: 607-722-5857), or Fax 1-800-895-0582 (outside US/Canada: 607-771-0012), or e-mail at:

getinfo@haworthpressinc.com

Caring on the Streets: A Study of Detached Youthworkers, Jacquelyn Kay Thompson, PhD (Vol. 19, No. 2 1999).

Boarding Schools at the Crossroads of Change: The Influence of Residential Education Institutions on National and Societal Development, Yitzhak Kashti, PhD (Vol. 19, No. 1, 1998). *"This book is an essential, applicable historical reference for those interested in positively molding the social future of the world's troubled youth."* *(Juvenile and Family Court Journal)*

The Occupational Experience of Residential Child and Youth Care Workers: Caring and Its Discontents, Edited by Mordecai Arieli, PhD (Vol. 18 No. 2, 1997). *"Introduces the social reality of residential child and youth care as viewed by care workers, examining the problem of tension between workers and residents and how workers cope with stress."* *(Book News, Inc.)*

The Anthropology of Child and Youth Care Work, Edited by Rivka A. Eisikovits, PhD (Vol. 18, No. 1, 1996). *"A fascinating combination of rich ethnographies from the occupational field of residential child and youth care and the challenging social paradigm of cultural perspective."* *(Mordecai Arieli, PhD, Senior Teacher, Educational Policy and Organization Department, Tel-Aviv University, Israel)*

Travels in the Trench Between Child Welfare Theory and Practice: A Case Study of Failed Promises and Prospects for Renewal, George Thomas, PhD, MSW (Vol. 17, No. 1/2, 1994). *"Thomas musters enough research and common sense to blow any proponent out of the water. . . . Here is a person of real integrity, speaking the sort of truth that makes self-serving administrators and governments quail."* *(Australian New Zealand Journal of Family Therapy)*

Negotiating Positive Identity in a Group Care Community: Reclaiming Uprooted Youth, Zvi Levy (Vol. 16, No. 2, 1993). *"This book will interest theoreticians, practitioners, and policymakers in child and youth care, teachers, and rehabilitation counselors. Recommended for academic and health science center library collections."* *(Academic Library Book Review)*

Information Systems in Child, Youth, and Family Agencies: Planning, Implementation, and Service Enhancement, Edited by Anthony J. Grasso, DSW, and Irwin Epstein, PhD (Vol. 16, No. 1, 1993). *"Valuable to anyone interested in the design and the implementation of a Management Information System (MIS) in a social service agency. . . ."* *(John G. Orme, PhD, Associate Professor, College of Social Work, University of Tennessee)*

Assessing Child Maltreatment Reports: The Problem of False Allegations, Edited by Michael Robin, MPH, ACSW (Vol. 15, No. 2, 1991). *"A thoughtful contribution to the public debate about how to fix the beleaguered system . . . . It should also be required reading in courses in child welfare."* (Science Books & Films)

People Care in Institutions: A Conceptual Schema and Its Application, Edited by Yochanan Wozner, DSW (Vol. 14, No. 2, 1990). *"Provides ample information by which the effectiveness of internats and the life of staff and internees can be improved."* (Residential Treatment for Children & Youth)

Being in Child Care: A Journey Into Self, Edited by Gerry Fewster, PhD (Vol. 14, No. 2 1990). *"Evocative and provocative. Reading this absolutely compelling work provides a transformational experience in which one finds oneself alternately joyful, angry, puzzled, illuminated, warmed, chilled."* (Karen VanderVen, PhD, Professor, Program in Child Development and Child Care, School of Social Work, University of Pittsburgh)

Homeless Children: The Watchers and the Waiters, Edited by Nancy Boxill, PhD (Vol. 14, No. 1, 1990). *"Fill[s] a gap in the popular and professional literature on homelessness . . . . Policymakers, program developers, and social welfare practitioners will find it particulary useful."* (Science Books & Films)

Perspectives in Professional Child and Youth Care, Edited by James P. Anglin, MSW, Carey J. Denholm, PhD, Roy V. Ferguson, PhD, and Alan R. Pence, PhD (Vol. 13, No. 1/2, 1990). *"Reinforced by empirical research and clear conceptual thinking, as well as the recognition of the relevance of personal transformation in understanding quality care."* (Virginia Child Protection Newsletter)

Specialist Foster Family Care: A Normalizing Experience, Edited by Burt Galaway, PhD, MS, and Joe Hudson, PhD, MSW (Vol. 12, No. 1/2, 1989). *"A useful and practical book for policymakers and professionals interested in learning about the benefits of treatment foster care."* (Ira M. Schwartz, MSW, Professor and Director, Center for the Study of Youth Policy, The University of Michigan School of Social Work)

Helping the Youthful Offender: Individual and Group Therapies That Work, William B. Lewis, PhD (Vol. 11, No. 2, 1991). *"In a reader-friendly and often humorous style, Lewis explains the multilevel approach that he deems necessary for effective treatment of delinquents within an institutional context."* (Criminal Justice Review)

Family Perspectives in Child and Youth Services, Edited by David H. Olson, PhD (Vol. 11, No. 1, 1989). *"An excellent diagnostic tool to use with families and an excellent training tool for our family therapy students. . . . It also offers an excellent model for parent training."* (Peter Maynard, PhD, Department of Human Development, University of Rhode Island)

Transitioning Exceptional Children and Youth Into the Community: Research and Practice, Edited by Ennio Cipani, PhD (Vol. 10, No. 2, 1989). *"Excellent set of chapters. A very fine contribution to the literature. Excellent text."* (T. F. McLaughlin, PhD, Department of Special Education, Gonzaga University)

Assaultive Youth: Responding to Physical Assaultiveness in Residential, Community, and Health Care Settings, Edited by Joel Kupfersmid, PhD, and Roberta Monkman, PhD (Vol. 10, No. 1, 1988). *"At last here is a book written by professionals who do direct care with assaultive youth and can give practical advice."* (Vicki L. Agee, PhD, Director of Correctional Services, New Life Youth Services, Lantana, Florida)

Developmental Group Care of Children and Youth: Concepts and Practice, Henry W. Maier, PhD (Vol. 9, No. 2, 1988). *"An excellent guide for those who plan to devote their professional careers to the group care of children and adolescents."* (Journal of Developmental and Behavioral Pediatrics)

The Black Adolescent Parent, Edited by Stanley F. Battle, PhD, MPH (Vol. 9, No. 1, 1987). *"A Sound and insightful perspective on black adolescent sexuality and parenting."* (Child Welfare)

Qualitative Research and Evaluation in Group Care, Edited by Rivka A. Eisikovits, PhD, and Yitzhak Kashti, PhD (Vol. 8, No. 3/4, 1987). *"Well worth reading. . . . should be read by any nurse involved in formally evaluating her care setting."* (Nursing Times)

Helping Delinquents Change: A Treatment Manual of Social Learning Approaches, Jerome S. Stumphauzer, PhD (Vol. 8, No. 1/2, 1986). *"The best I have seen in the juvenile and criminal justice field in the past 46 years. It is pragmatic and creative in its recommended treatment approaches, on target* *concerning the many aspects of juvenile handling that have failed, and quite honest in assessing and advocating which practices seem to be working reasonably well." (Corrections Today)*

Residential Group Care in Community Context: Insights from the Israeli Experience, Edited by Zvi Eisikovits, PhD, and Jerome Beker, EdD (Vol. 7, No. 3/4, 1986). *A variety of highly effective group care settings in Israel are examined, with suggestions for improving care in the United States.*

Adolescents, Literature, and Work with Youth, Edited by J. Pamela Weiner, MPH, and Ruth M. Stein, PhD (Vol. 7, No. 1/2, 1985). *"A variety of thought-provoking ways of looking at adolescent literature." (Harvard Educational Review)*

Young Girls: A Portrait of Adolescence, Reprint Edition, Gisela Konopka, DSW (Vol. 6, No. 3/4, 1985). *"A sensitive affirmation of today's young women and a clear recognition of the complex adjustments they face in contemporary society." (School Counselor)*

Adolescent Substance Abuse: A Guide to Prevention and Treatment, Edited by Richard E. Isralowitz and Mark Singer (Vol. 6, No. 1/2, 1983). *"A Valuable tool for those working with as adolescent substance misusers." (Journal of Studies on Alcohol)*

Social Skills Training for Children and Youth, Edited by Craig LeCroy, MSW (Vol. 5, No. 3/4, 1983). *"Easy to read and pertinent to occupational therapists." (New Zealand Journal of Occupational Therapy)*

Legal Reforms Affecting Child and Youth Services, Edited by Gary B. Melton, PhD (Vol. 5, No. 1/2, 1983). *"A consistently impressive book. The authors bring a wealth of empirical data and creative legal analyses to bear on one of the most important topics in psychology and law." (John Monahan, School of Law, University of Virginia)*

Youth Participation and Experiential Education, Edited by Daniel Conrad and Diane Hedin (Vol. 4, No. 3/4, 1982). *A useful introduction and overview of the current and possible future impact of experiential education on adolescents.*

Institutional Abuse of Children and Youth, Edited by Ranae Hanson (Vol. 4, No. 1/2, 1982). *"Well researched... should be required reading for every school administrator, school board member, teacher, and parent." (American Psychological Association Division 37 Newsletter)*

Caring on the Streets:
A Study
of Detached Youthworkers

Jacquelyn Kay Thompson

Caring on the Streets: A Study of Detached Youthworkers has been co-published simultaneously as *Child & Youth Services*, Volume 19, Number 2 1999.

The Haworth Press, Inc.
New York • London • Oxford

Caring on the Streets: A Study of Detached Youthworkers has been co-published simultaneously as *Child & Youth Services,* ™ Volume 19, Number 2 1999.

Cover design by Thomas J. Mayshock Jr.

The Haworth Press, Inc., 10 Alice Street, Binghamton, NY 13904-1580 USA

Library of Congress Cataloging-in-Publication Data

Thompson, Jacquelyn Kay.
Caring on the streets: a study of detached youthworkers / Jacquelyn Kay Thompson.
    p. cm.
    "Co-published simultaneously as Child & youth services, volume 19, number 2 1999."
    Includes bibliographical references and index.
    ISBN 0-7890-0781-9 (alk. paper)–ISBN 0-7890-0816-5 (alk. paper)
    1. Social work with youth. 2. Social work with youth–Methodology. I. Title.
HV1421 .T47 1999
362.7'083–dc21
                                                99-051403
                                                      CIP

INDEXING & ABSTRACTING

Contributions to this publication are selectively indexed or abstracted in print, electronic, online, or CD-ROM version(s) of the reference tools and information services listed below. This list is current as of the copyright date of this publication. See the end of this section for additional notes.

- *BUBL Information Service. An Internet-based Information Service for the UK higher education community*

- *Cambridge Scientific Abstracts*

- *Child Development Abstracts & Bibliography*

- *CNPIEC Reference Guide: Chinese National Directory of Foreign Periodicals*

- *Criminal Justice Abstracts*

- *ERIC Clearinghouse on Counseling and Student Services (ERIC/CASS)*

- *ERIC Clearinghouse on Elementary & Early Childhood Education*

- *Exceptional Child Education Resources (ECER), (CD/ROM from SilverPlatter and hard copy)*

- *Family Studies Database (online and CD/ROM)*

- *IBZ International Bibliography of Periodical Literature*

- *Index to Periodical Articles Related to Law*

- *International Bulletin of Bibliography on Education*
- *Mental Health Abstracts (online through DIALOG)*

- *National Center for Chronic Disease Prevention & Health Promotion (NCCDPHP)*
- *National Criminal Justice Reference Services*
- *OT BibSys*
- *PASCAL , c/o Institute de L'information Scientifique et Technique. Cross-Disciplinary electronic database covering the fields of science, technology & medicine. Also available on CD-ROM, and can generate customized retrospective searches. For more information: INIST, Customer Desk, 2, allec du Parc de Brabois, F-154514 Vandoeuvere Cedex, France; http//www.inst.fr*

(continued)

- *Psychological Abstracts (PsycINFO)*
- *Referativnyi Zhurnal (Abstracts Journal of the Institute of Scientific Information of the Republic of Russia)*
- *Sage Family Studies Abstracts (SFSA)*
- *Social Planning/Policy & Development Abstracts (SOPODA)*
- *Social Sciences Index*
- *Social Work Abstracts*
- *Sociological Abstracts (SA)*
- *Sociology of Education Abstracts*
- *Studies on Women Abstracts*
- *Violence and Abuse Abstracts: A Review of Current Literature on Interpersonal Violence (VAA)*

Special Bibliographic Notes related to special journal issues (separates) and indexing/abstracting:

- indexing/abstracting services in this list will also cover material in any "separate" that is co-published simultaneously with Haworth's special thematic journal issue or DocuSerial. Indexing/abstracting usually covers material at the article/chapter level.
- monographic co-editions are intended for either non-subscribers or libraries which intend to purchase a second copy for their circulating collections.
- monographic co-editions are reported to all jobbers/wholesalers/approval plans. The source journal is listed as the "series" to assist the prevention of duplicate purchasing in the same manner utilized for books-in-series.
- to facilitate user/access services all indexing/abstracting services are encouraged to utilize the co-indexing entry note indicated at the bottom of the first page of each article/chapter/contribution.
- this is intended to assist a library user of any reference tool (whether print, electronic, online, or CD-ROM) to locate the monographic version if the library has purchased this version but not a subscription to the source journal.
- individual articles/chapters in any Haworth publication are also available through the Haworth Document Delivery Service (HDDS).

Setting the Stage

WE DON'T GET PAID
TO GO TO
FUNERALS, DELIVERIES,
GRADUATIONS, WEDDINGS
—BUT WE GO!

WE DON'T GET PAID ENOUGH
TO BE
JUMPED, YELLED AT, SLAPPED,
AND ARRESTED BY MISTAKE
—BUT WE ARE!

WE DON'T OFFICIALLY
GET REQUESTED
TO GET UP AT 3:00 AM
AND RESCUE SOME KID
—BUT WE GO!

WE ARE NOT ASKED TO
CRY, LAUGH, AND BE SCARED
FOR
AND WITH OUR CLIENTS
—BUT WE DO!

WE ARE OFTEN NOT RESPECTED
OR EVEN SEEN AS PROFESSIONAL,
BUT I GUESS THERE'S GOT TO BE SOME PRICE
—AFTER ALL,
ON HOW MANY JOBS CAN ONE GO TO WORK
IN JEANS AND TENNIS SHOES EVERYDAY?

-An experienced detached youthworker reflecting on her job

I would like to dedicate this book to the hundreds of kids who, throughout the years, allowed me to be a part of their lives; the kids who took time and were patient in teaching me how to do my job. They truly have given me every bit as much as I have given them and, at times, even more.

Caring on the Streets:
A Study
of Detached Youthworkers

CONTENTS

ABOUT THE AUTHOR

Jacquelyn Kay Thompson, PhD, is a clinical and counseling psychologist with degrees from Metro State University in St. Paul, the University of Wisconsin-River Falls, and Union Graduate School (Cincinnatti). A licensed consulting and school psychologist in Minnesota , she has published in *Children Today* and led research, evaluation, and demonstration projects focused on such areas as transitional housing for adolescents, school-based clinics, and adolescent prostitution. She is currently a psychologist with Family Visions, Inc., Fridley, Minnesota, having previously served with other agencies including Lutheran Social Services (St. Paul), the St. Paul Public Schools, the University of Minnesota, and the Mille Lacs Band of Ojibwe Native Americans. Throughout her career, her primary commitment has been to the practice and development of detached youthwork as a career-for herself and for others-in the service of young people in our society.

Foreword

I have known and worked closely with Jackie Thompson since 1972; as her doctoral advisor, I was present from the gestation to the successful delivery of her dissertation, on which this book is based. I have always been her student!

Jackie was the pre-eminent street youthworker in our area, and the one with the longest service in a worker role that invites both psychosocial and existential burnout. While she experienced both, she showed herself to be ever resilient and renewable because the young people and their worlds offered an invitation that she could never refuse. One of Jackie's first clients is now forty years old and making it as well as any of us.

For years and years, we spoke almost every night on the telephone about the day-what had happened, what had changed for whom, and what she had learned that day about youthwork, kids, the world, and other important "stuff." Her dissertation and this book came out of her life-world experiences with these street kids and with her many friends and colleagues throughout the local youth agency scene-among them Rev. Marvin Grunke of Lutheran Social Service, St. Paul, a mentor to many of us on how to be a good person while doing the right thing and her long time supervisor and friend. Jackie the person-as-youthworker became the action-scholar as she talked with other local street youthworkers in this first local study of their role.

When the field research was begun, the literature on street youthwork in the United States was primarily about detached youthwork with gangs in New York City, Los Angeles, and Chicago, while other writings were appearing in England (about streetwork with young men), in Israel (where the focus was on Jerusalem and the army's use of detached workers in slum areas), and in Latin America, (where the focus was on "street kids"-young people "*of* the streets" in contrast

[Haworth co-indexing entry note]: "Foreword." Baizerman, Michael. Co-published simultaneously in *Child & Youth Services* (The Haworth Press, Inc.) Vol. 19, No. 2, 1999, pp. xv-xviii; and: *Caring on the Streets: A Study of Detached Youthworkers* (Jacquelyn Kay Thompson) The Haworth Press, Inc., pp. xv-xviii. Single or multiple copies of this article are available for a fee from The Haworth Document Delivery Service [1-800-342-9678, 9:00 a.m. - 5:00 p.m. (EST). E-mail address: getinfo@haworthpressinc.com].

to the focus in the United States at that time on young people "*on* the streets"). Later, street youthwork in Australia and in various European and Asian countries expanded as a local response to teen gangs, delinquency, drug use, and AIDS classic "moral panics" about youth-as well as to countercultural and political youth movements (moral panics of a different kind).

As this work grew as a response to these situations (with concomitant increases in the number of workers and in the styles and forums of street/detached youthwork), a small but growing stream of articles appeared-often written by academics and agency professionals, not by front-line streetworkers. Unfortunately, as we know, most youthworkers do not write about their experiences for their colleagues, scholars, or "their kids," nor do they typically read much about youthwork. Thus, this text is unusual in part because it was written by an active street youthworker who became a worker-scholar and received formal education and training.

In the dead of night, I wonder, as does Jackie, whether the series of decisions she made to reflect, study, and write served to move her from the worlds wherein she was most at home to clinical work to pay the bills for her schooling, creating a person who was (at least at times) alienated from her vocational call. This is a site where the vocational self touches the occupational self and the wonderfully named phenomenon "trained incapacity"-being "fit in an unfit fitness" (Thorstein Veblen, I think).

At this historical moment, street youthwork is an accepted worker role, albeit a highly romanticized occupation. It surely is done "where the action is," while its practitioners forget that there is more than one kind and site of "action." Such youthwork is done "where kids are at"-both in the geographic place and world and "in their heads," their metaphoric place. Street youthwork is about these and related geographies of everyday life of certain groups of youth; it is about how geometric space becomes lived-space and the life-worlds of site, venue, and locale; and it is about how these geographies work as calls or invitations or addresses for some kids-as well as some adults, including youthworkers-and how they respond by taking on existing street roles or creating new ones specific as to age, sex, ethnicity/race, and social class, e.g., pimp, "ho," "gang banger," "wannabe," addict, and detached youthworker.

As a street youthworker, Jackie has worked the streets, bars, apartments, lofts, corners, pool halls, fast food places and "squats"-at the places and times when kids are always present (even if inaudible and invisible to the untutored ear and eye). Present in her text are the workers, detached and agency-based, as well; an attentive reader will hear all of this.

Research about youthworkers by an especially gifted youthworker has familiar methodological problems, which the researcher here controls in part by bracketing her experiences and certainties to allow the other person's worlds and self to be told. More special is the way she co-creates the interview/visit and thus the resulting text/transcript, thus opening for reflection this increasingly acceptable strategy of exploration and personal transformation. The content and Jackie's thematic analysis brought the themes forward and thus made them available for reflection by herself, by other interviewees, and by her readers. Her phenomenological research strategy is now in vogue in the United States as well as in some other countries; a few years ago, when she did the research, it was innovative.

Also unusual then and less so now is her attentiveness to the American distinctions between *knowing* and *doing* and between *doing* and *being*. The first pair is brought together in professional praxis and the second in the self. In the United States, *doing* drives *being*, with involvement in activities thought to lead to "development" and to "character." But activities can lead to more activities, fun, joy, and skill, yet not "produce" a good person. The moral is thematic in all of this, and Jackie struggles to join the "right thing to do, rightly, to the "good way to be." She uses the notion of vocation to get at all this and at the source of some workers' commitment to the kids and to their ways of doing youthwork.

Jackie's study reflected our youthwork community in its commitment to and search for the stuff of practice. This was a source of my own four-year study of vocation and youth development (Baizerman, 1998), a theme also in the studies of youthwork she cites by two of our students, Tania Chalhub-Oliveira (1995) and Walter deOliveira (1994) (unrelated), both of Brazil. And it portrays as well the relative inarticulateness of many streetworkers (and many kids); without words, we poorly name our worlds, our lived-realities, and our modes-of-being, and we may not achieve a fully-flourishing existence. This is not an elitist claim, nor does it exclude the many alternate ways of saying self and work, and of giving voice. Rather, it brings attention to the fact that many youthworkers do not know "what they are doing" and/or how to talk about their work.

In our locale, street youthwork has become a "way of response," in Buber's phrase (Glatzer, 1966), for some youthworkers who are lesbian to find a way to work with youth and even to create a new youthwork without being demonized for their personal, ethical sexual relationships. The Romantic myth of "streetwork" has been blended into a fashion and a lifestyle. These at first seem to be subcultural forms of resistance to youth agency norms of worker style, dress, and demeanor-and for some they are, but not for all: ethical, professional street youthworkers come in all sizes, shapes, and colors. A keen reader will notice these.

Jackie was a worker "guru," others said, and here again she is our teacher. She could not be and do otherwise! And it is this that we witness and honor in this Foreword.

Michael Baizerman
University of Minnesota

Acknowledgments

I was advised not to include a thank-you page because "you will inevitably forget to mention someone." After some thought on this, I have come to a truth. I did not write this paper or even get through the process without a lot of help, support, understanding, and energy from a lot of people. It would be arrogant and dishonest (at the very least) not to acknowledge that. So I have attempted to thank everyone, with the understanding that I have inevitably forgot someone.

I would like to start by thanking the youthworkers for their time and openness, without which none of this could have happened. I would especially like to thank the youthworkers who were then at Lutheran Social Services (St. Paul): Chris, Don, and Dennis–not only because they have been a great team of people to work with, but also because they were willing to listen and give their honest opinions throughout the process. Special thanks to T. C. for inspiring the title of this book.

I also appreciate the cooperation and support of Lutheran Social Services for giving me a sabbatical leave so that I could complete the interviews. A special thanks to Ellen Erickson for being a supportive and wise mentor and supervisor.

I owe a great deal to the people at the Center for Youth Development and Research–now the Youth Studies Program–at the University of Minnesota. The staff have been a source of ongoing support. I am especially grateful for their willingness to share their time, wisdom, and influence through the years. Special thanks to Jerry Beker and Irl Carter, Mike Baizerman, Judith Erickson, Mary Burnison, and Beth Emshoff.

Special thanks also to St. Paul Companies and Mary Pickard and Polly Nygard for believing in me and for their commitment to youth.

To Michael Patton, Willson Williams, Ira Lourie, Michael Baizerman, Dennis Conroy, and Elizabeth Palmer, my sincere thanks for their constructive input, time, and energy as members of the committee that supervised my dissertation, on which this book is based.

I am grateful to Lynn Powers for serving as an evaluator and clinical supervisor and for being such a great resource throughout this process. To Joan Hiller, thanks for the hours spent with me "processing" and rethinking things.

It is with deep gratitude that I acknowledge Marv Grunke–for believing in all this and in me from the very beginning.

I am extremely grateful to Mike Baizerman; he has been my mentor, my youthworker, and my friend through the years. He has always been willing to share his way of seeing and being–open for true dialogue.

My ongoing appreciation and gratitude to my parents, Sig and Geri Thompson, my sister, Debbie Boehm, and to Stan and Angie Podobinski, Mary Podobinski, and Nancy Martinson, for their constant encouragement and financial support.

To my nieces, Cori and Jami Boehm, I am thankful for the walks and talks, but especially thankful and proud of who they are.

A thank you to Tasha and Ari Baizerman and Dougie and Angie Smith for always offering another way to see things.

To Mary and Nancy: thank you for the hours of typing, proofreading and for still remaining friends.

To Cindy and Doris, a special thanks for the library runs, reading, and support.

I have a special appreciation for Diane Olson, who listened for hours and who pushed, pulled, and at times carried me through this process. Thank you.

To Poodie, Bertha, Elsie, Misha, Willie, Pumpkin, Saki, Princess, Lillie, Mattie, Agatha, Christie, Tumbleweed, Buber and even Kahuna, O. B., and Stagger-Lee for giving the understanding and joy that only they can give.

To all who I have mentioned and to those I forgot, thank you for understanding and accepting my, "I can't, I don't have time," as an answer to you during the study and the preparation of this book.

Jackie

Chapter I

Introduction

Caring on the Streets: A Study of Detached Youthworkers

"I'm sorry, but David died in surgery." I sat there, and I could feel the numbness taking over my body. I looked at the doctor, then over at the 19-year-old mother. I didn't say anything; I didn't know what to say. I just sat there feeling numb. He was a two-year-old, quite skinny, cute little boy. I flashed back: I remembered when he was born–I called him Big Foot. He had the biggest feet. Six months before, I had been in the hospital with him and his sister reporting child abuse. Now he was dead, beaten to death by Mom's boyfriend. I'd known the mom for about three years. She had been beaten by this boyfriend and by every boyfriend before him, as well as by many of her customers and by her father. I walked out into the lobby and saw that the police were the same ones who had been called six months ago.

I walked over to one of them. I looked at him and said, "We really f----- this one up." "Now come on, Jackie," he replied, "we all did our best." We all did our best and we still have a dead two-year-old–I couldn't buy that. "Look, Jackie, think of all the kids you've saved."

It didn't seem to matter right then. I cried all the way home from the hospital and spent the next three days and nights going through every event, every meeting, every conversation, going through every "should have" and "could have." I ended up taking the next six weeks off.

* * *

I walked into the house with the kid. She had skipped school and was scared to go home and face her dad alone–so I went home with

---

[Haworth co-indexing entry note]: "Introduction." Thompson, Jacquelyn Kay. Co-published simultaneously in *Child & Youth Services* (The Haworth Press, Inc.) Vol. 19, No. 2, 1999, pp. 1-6; and: *Caring on the Streets: A Study of Detached Youthworkers* (Jacquelyn Kay Thompson) The Haworth Press, Inc., 1999, pp. 1-6. Single or multiple copies of this article are available for a fee from The Haworth Document Delivery Service [1-800-342-9678, 9:00 a.m. - 5:00 p.m. (EST). E-mail address: getinfo@haworthpressinc.com].

her. We sat at the kitchen table while she told him. He jumped up and started beating her–I asked him to stop and, when he didn't, I stepped between them. He grabbed me, and I just stood there with my eyes shut waiting for the blow. He must have suddenly realized what he was doing and let go of me. My heart was pounding.

* * *

We went into the apartment to get the kid and when we got there, she was high and passed out on the couch. I went over to try to get her, and her pimp came into the room screaming: "What are you two bitches doing in my apartment?" My partner yelled back at him: "We're taking her with us, so just back off!"

At first I didn't see him pull out the gun, but I heard my partner start to change her tone. So he has this gun pointed at us and said, "I could blow both of you away and say you were breaking and entering."

* * *

She called at about 3 a.m. to say she was in this motel. I could tell she was really high and knew she was turning tricks. I asked her if she had Norrel (her one-year-old son) with her and she said, "Yes, he is asleep." I told her I would come and pick him up. So I went and got the baby and brought him home with me. He had to sleep in a dresser drawer, and in the morning I had to find a place to bring him, then go and find his mother and deal with her.

* * *

She called and said she wanted to leave "the business" and her pimp, but she was in Milwaukee and had no way to get herself and her two kids home. I called all over trying to find transportation and/or money to get them back here, but there was nothing. So "after work" I left, drove to Milwaukee, picked them up, and brought them home.

* * *

Her mom was dying; she had cancer. The hospital had called and said, "You have about three hours to find her daughter if she is going to see her mom alive." The daughter had been in and out of prostitution for two years, but she and her mother really loved each other. I had known the family for about three years and had gone through this when her father had died the previous year, also of cancer, and I knew it would be important for them to see each other. I went out onto the streets to look for her.

It took me about two hours, but I found her, and when we got to the hospital and walked into her mom's room, the woman looked up and smiled. "I knew you'd get here," she said weakly. I was going to walk out of the room when she called for me. I went to her bedside and she held my hand and looked very peaceful and said, "Promise me you will watch over her–she is a good girl." I looked at her and smiled. "I promise." "Thank you," she said, "thank you for everything."

After that I left so she could be alone with her daughter. About twenty minutes later she died. Her daughter and I left the hospital and walked and talked for the next three hours. I spent a lot of time with her for the following three days: The wake, the funeral, and the lonely time afterward. I think I'll know this kid for the rest of my life.

* * *

She called crying. She said she had been raped. I got her to tell me where she was, and I picked her up and took her to the hospital. I spent the next two hours fighting with the hospital staff, trying to explain that a "hooker" could be raped!

* * *

I sat there on the corner talking to him. He would jump into a car and turn a trick. I'd wait, then he'd come back and we'd talk some more. I had just met him so I was making light conversation, but after about an hour I decided to go into my AIDS talk. I asked him if he knew about AIDS; he said "Yeah, I know." I asked him if he had concerns about getting AIDS and he said he had tested positive; he had gotten the results yesterday.

* * *

I don't know how many times they've said, "We don't have money for raises." Most of the time they aren't sure we'll even have a program in six months.

* * *

It's hard to sign a mortgage for thirty years when you don't know if your program is even funded for next year.

*   *   *

All my clients make more money than I do. Crime pays, and it pays damn well!

*   *   *

At staffings I don't really say anything. I mean, they have all these social workers and psychologists. They don't listen to youthworkers. We don't have any power, and in most cases we don't even have their respect.

*   *   *

It seems like in the fall and around the holidays, I don't have one day to myself. I have to take my phone off the hook just to find a minute to be alone.

*   *   *

I am always fighting or wanting to fight systems–or wanting to be able to quit fighting the system.

*   *   *

If it's a profession, then the professional hazard is heartbreak!

*   *   *

The price that a detached youthworker pays to wear tennis shoes to work is heard in these stories and comments. This study was begun with the idea of looking into how detached youthworkers *experience* being a youthworker in an attempt to answer the question, "What is detached youthwork and how is it practiced?" No study was found in the literature that looked at youthwork from the perspective of the worker. This is done here with total awareness that one may be able to address or describe an experience, but one can never fully explain or understand it.

I remember visiting the Grand Canyon about two years ago. I stood on the edge of the canyon and was in total awe of its magnificence: the colors, the depth, the "bigger than life" quality of it all. It was a spiritual experience. I grabbed my camera and proceeded to snap one picture after another. I can remember my disappointment when I got the pictures back. They just didn't seem to capture the essence of standing on the edge of the canyon: The wind, the smells, the mood and feelings that were present there. What was captured in the pictures was a representation of that experience, an abstraction.

It is with that insight and understanding that I have attempted to describe what I have heard and experienced within the last year of listening to youthworkers. I hope that I have captured at least an accurate picture of their experience.

It is also with this understanding that it became clear that the approach that could best capture the essence of youthwork was one using phenomenological psychology, for phenomenological psychology emphasizes the study of experience. Colaizzi (1973) says that "experience is an irreducible phenomenon and is the source of all human significance without which there would be no meaning whatsoever" (p. 5). The study could have been done using quantitative methods: one might administer a number of personality tests, such as the *California Personality Inventory,* the *Myers-Briggs Type Indicator,* and/or the *Minnesota Multiphasic Personality Inventory,* etc., as well as a number of occupational tests (e.g., *Kuder Preference Record*) along with time-motion studies and detailed activity logs. The results would be clear measures–"hard" data–but we would not have an understanding of the essentials of youthwork. As Maslow (1960) said so eloquently: "We measure everything and understand nothing" (p. 54).

The phenomenological approach is how I choose to look at the world, and I took an existential stance. "Meaning is the measurement" (Maslow, 1960, p. 55). Meaning has been my way of understanding (i.e., measurement) and has been the way in which I have worked and lived for the past 17 years, if not for my whole life. For example, I spent three years "hanging out on the streets" to understand kids involved in prostitution–talking with them, asking questions that would lead to an understanding of their reality, their sense of their alternatives and options (choices), their sense of their world. A program was then developed based on those understandings. During the last 14 years, I have been "on the street" letting kids teach me how to be helpful to them.

The following statement speaks not only to my experience in doing this study, but to my experience of just about everything that I have come to know (for today):

> Initially one must assume more than one knows and only during the process of the research itself does one become more fully

aware of precisely what it is that one knows and why what one knows must be so. Thus, the later phases deepen and transform the earlier phases but they could not have achieved what they did except by means of the earlier phases. (Kiesow, 1973, p. 79)

It is with this sense of tentativeness that I offer this as an early phase of the ongoing process of learning and understanding youthwork–and perhaps as a "later phase" in my personal understanding.

I took on exploring *Caring on the Streets: A Study of Detached Youthworkers* with the belief that there are better and/or easier ways to select, train, and supervise youthworkers. I trust that this study will contribute to that end.

Chapter II

The Literature–
What Have Others Taught Us?

To answer the research question "What is detached youthwork and how is it practiced?" it is necessary first to know the history of youthwork. Literature dealing with detached youthwork is found in law, sociology, psychology, social work, criminal justice, and in the popular press. Information on youthwork in the United States is the focus here, although there is extensive relevant literature in Europe, Great Britain, and in the Latin American countries as well. While the foreign literature is not reviewed here in depth, it becomes significant in considering the implications of this study and will be referred to in this context in the conclusions.

From the mid 1960s until the present there has been very little published in the United States on detached youthworkers or detached youthwork programs. Baizerman (e.g., 1979, 1980, 1981, and 1982) has published several articles on various aspects of detached youthwork and detached youthworkers, and the journal *Child & Youth Services* covers much that is applicable to the field of detached youthwork (e.g., Anglin, Denholm, Ferguson, & Pence, 1990). This literature searches for the moral and existential source of day-to-day youthwork in the process of focusing on normalcy and hope.

There are a number of possible explanations for the paucity of literature about detached youthwork since the late 1960s. First, detached youthwork was no longer a new, exciting approach to dealing with gangs. It had been around for twenty years and it worked, accord-

[Haworth co-indexing entry note]: "The Literature–What Have Others Taught Us?" Thompson, Jacquelyn Kay. Co-published simultaneously in *Child & Youth Services* (The Haworth Press, Inc.) Vol. 19, No. 2, 1999, pp. 7-33; and: *Caring on the Streets: A Study of Detached Youthworkers* (Jacquelyn Kay Thompson) The Haworth Press, Inc., 1999, pp. 7-33. Single or multiple copies of this article are available for a fee from The Haworth Document Delivery Service [1-800-342-9678, 9:00 a.m. - 5:00 p.m. (EST). E-mail address: getinfo@haworthpressinc.com].

ing to those in the field (e.g., New York City Youth Board, 1952). However, no one had developed a solid theory of detached youthwork, no established discipline claimed it as its own, and there was no consensus regarding the roles and knowledge base of detached youthwork.

Second, the nature of gang behavior shifted from one of public fighting and the terrorizing of neighbors, to one which was more private and involved in drugs. For example, the New York City Youth Board (1985) noted this shift beginning and said "new demands of narcotic addiction, school and employment are replacing fights as the focal point of the gang's concern" (p. 58). Hence, gangs tend to be less visible and are seen by the public as less troublesome, with some exceptions, although this may now be changing in the face of seemingly increased gang violence largely related to involvement in the illegal drug business.

Thus, a third possible explanation is that the behavior of adolescent gang members had been viewed by many as "normal" until the late 1960s (e.g., Cloward and Ohlin, 1960; Kvaraceus & Miller, 1959), when the conception changed from that of a societal problem ("social issue") to one in which the youth were seen as troubled or psychologically disturbed ("personal problems"). Social concern also shifted from the lower class adolescent to the middle class adolescent, with the "flower child" movement, the Vietnam War protests, and the civil rights movement. Finally, youthworkers did not develop a literature because of their biases against scholarly work, including research about their practices and "their kids."

The literature reviewed includes adolescent gangs because they were the raison d'etre for creating detached youthwork; early programs of detached youthwork because they set the tone for later programs; and the nitty-gritty of detached youthwork itself.

THEORY AND HISTORY OF JUVENILE DELINQUENCY AND JUVENILE GANGS

To best understand detached youthwork and its source in youth gangwork, one must first look at juvenile gangs and the larger context of juvenile delinquency. It is from this that detached youthwork developed.

To the scholar of the late 1950s to the mid-1960s, juvenile delinquency was a growth industry. Among the many early writings, the works of Shaw (e.g., Shaw & Jacobs, 1940) and the "Chicago School" had a significant impact on subsequent work with youth. Shaw found that delinquency and crime tended to be confined to delimited areas and that the delinquent behavior persisted despite demographic changes in these areas. He spoke of "criminal tradition" and the "cultural transmission" of criminal values. In this tradition, "delinquency, for the most part (was) seen as a reversible accident of the person's social experience" (Kobrin, 1959, p. 22).

Cloward and Ohlin (1960) expanded the notion of "cultural trans-mission" and argued that delinquency arises because opportunities are blocked to lower class youth who want the same things as other youth but cannot find socially legitimate ways to achieve these goals. Gang activity becomes a viable way for them to achieve "success." One way is by moving into juvenile criminal activity, a second is proving one's manhood through fighting, while a third is giving up and retreat-ing into chemical use.

A third theory, the Cultural Approach (e.g., Kvaraceus and Miller, 1959) looked at lower-class neighborhoods as having developed rela-tively stable subcultures in which certain criminal and delinquent values and behavior were accepted as normative. Lerner (1957) pro-posed a fourth theory that looks at delinquency as a manifestation of the general breakdown in community standards, i.e., social disorgani-zation.

A fifth approach was psychogenic. In it, the adolescent's family and early childhood experiences were seen as predictive of later troubles (e.g., Aichhorn, 1935; Redl, 1945). Another perspective was "rites of passage" (e.g., Bloch & Niederhoffer, 1958). Here, delinquency was seen as a normal process, that some adolescents pass through on their way to adulthood. Finally, a seventh approach saw delinquency from a situational perspective in which youth were viewed as "acting out" as a way of reducing personal tensions. This approach, too, shows an obvious psychological-psychiatric theory base, and some have sug-gested biological linkages as well.

Bernstein (1964) subscribed to a multiple causation model. He claimed that "delinquency is not a unitary diagnostic category. It is behavior which is in conflict with the law within a designated age range. Its origins are diverse not only from one youth to another but also within any one youngster" (p. 25).

Theoretical Perspectives on Adolescent Gangs

Implicitly and often explicitly, the early view of youth gangs was to see them as a normal manifestation of adolescent development. Basic to this view was a conception of delinquency and delinquents as "normal," i.e., not pathological, although maybe not "typical," i.e., delinquency as socially "deviant." For example, Thrasher (1927) said:

> Gangs represent the spontaneous effort of boys to create a society for themselves where none adequate to their needs exist . . . the failure of normally directing and controlling customs and institutions to function efficiently in the boy's experience is indicated by disintegration of life, inefficiency of schools, formalism and externality of religion, corruption and indifference in local politics, low wages and monotony in occupational activities, unemployment, and lack of opportunity for wholesome recreation. (p. 37)

Or Freeman (1956):

> . . . phenomena of the corner crowd is a natural function of the situation . . . (p. 15).

Lerman (1958) explicitly stated that to understand gang behavior, one must consider factors other than personality dynamics. These include:

> The internal relationships of the group and the evolved roles, status, structure, norms, and persistency of interaction of the individual's immediate peer group; the pressures toward conformity and the potentiating effects of group participation, predominant values of the significant people and institutions within the neighborhood life space affecting the individual and his primary reference group; the mode and style of personal controls of behavior prescribed, permitted, and proscribed by outside sources, and the reality aspects of the specific problem situation with which the individual is confronted. (pp. 71-72)

Gangwork

The number of articles in the literature on gangs and gang behavior declined in the mid-1960s. Campbell (1984) comments on this phenomenon in her book on girls and gangs:

In the Sixties, for example, it was widely believed that . . . gangs had finally disappeared. Absorbed into youth politics, some argued. Fighting in Vietnam, said others, or turned into self-destructive junkies. It seems likely that their disappearance was a media sleight of hand. New York stopped reporting gang stories and the rest of the country followed suit. Gangs die out and are reincarnated regularly by the media whenever news is slow. As a phenomenon, they have never been fully put to rest. When gangs return, they are not reinvented. Though they may be inactive for a few months or a few years, they are quietly living in the tradition and culture that has sustained them for over a hundred years in the United States. (pp. 5-6)

The popular press has again picked up on gangs in the 1990s, and many articles have been published (e.g., *Time,* February 19, 1990, June 18, 1990; *Jet,* January 15, 1990; *Minneapolis-St. Paul Magazine,* May 1990). The *Star Tribune* (Sunday, July 22, 1990), the major newspaper of the largest metropolitan area in Minnesota, carried a front page article on gangs in the Twin Cities and, as if to prove Ms. Campbell's point, stated that:

> *Five years ago* [italics mine], when gangs first surfaced in the Twin Cities, it was estimated that there were between 25 and 30 members and their activities were limited to misdemeanor crimes such as theft and vandalism. Today, police . . . have identified more than 3,000 gang members; they now deal in drugs and violence. (p. 12A)

Yet a review of earlier articles in the same newspaper found that gangs and gang behavior were the object of front page articles as far back as the mid-1950s (e.g., August 9, September 11, and October 1, 1957; September 1, 1959, November 7, 1963). Articles in the media, while not explicitly stating it, look at gang activity as did Cloward and Ohlin in 1960. For example, according to *Time* magazine (June 18, 1990),

> . . . inner-city youth of Los Angeles, at the center of the most advanced society on earth, respond to adversity and deprivation by regressing to a primitive parody of tribes. (p. 52)

Given the predominant early view that juvenile delinquency arose out of conditions in society and that gangs were a "natural consequence" of such conditions and of adolescent development, and yet were troublesome to society, it is not surprising that social service agencies, churches, and leisure time organizations attempted to involve gang members in their programs. Thrasher (1927) described this early work:

> In the early 1920s businesses, the YMCA, the Boy Scouts, the settlements, the parks and the playgrounds, and the Boys Clubs attempted to take over the gangs and turn them into social or athletic clubs. The politicians and the saloon keepers have also learned the trick of taking over these gangs and making clubs out of them, but their motives have usually been rather more for their own aggrandizement than for the good of the boys. (pp. 509-510)

However, these programs were unable to draw the boys in or, when they did come, they were disruptive and seen as a "threat" to others (Thrasher, 1927).

As a response to this failure to incorporate the boys into their ongoing programs, settlement houses and early leisure-time agencies probably sent some workers into the community. However, this was not done systematically, was not called detached youthwork, probably involved the use of indigenous young men, and was focused on involving male adolescents in organized athletic activities (Thrasher, 1927). Some of the neighborhood associations affiliated with the Chicago Area Project in the early 1930s used detached youthworkers but again did not initially call them this. Kobrin (1959), in a 25-year assessment of the Chicago Area Project, stated that,

> In all probability, the Area Project was the first organized program in the United States to use workers to establish direct and personal contact with the "unreached" boys. (p. 27)

Explicit Detached Youthwork Programs

It was not until World War II, when there was an increase in adolescent delinquent gangs, that more attention was given to them. One response to the emergence and recognition of gangs was to create detached worker programs, which appeared almost simultaneously in many large cities as social service agencies and units of government came to recognize that traditional, building-centered programs were ineffective in controlling and preventing gang disruption (Kobrin, 1959, New York City Youth Board, 1965). One study done in 1947 reported that fewer than 10% of the problem youth were attending in-building programs (Dumpson, 1949).

The terms "detached youthworker," "gang worker," "area worker," "streetworker," "corner-worker," "corner-group worker," "extension worker," and "street gang worker" were descriptions of where these workers did their work and whom they worked with.[1]

Lerman (1958) provided a succinct definition that fits most detached worker programs reviewed here:

> A non-membership, community located, professional service provided through a single worker who works in an environmental situation over which s/he has limited control and who extends service to a group without prior request from them for service. (p. 45)

A more comprehensive definition comes from the Boston Special Youth Project (Freeman, 1956):

> Detached work involves intensive contact with a corner-group where the worker meets the teen-age group in their natural environment. By close association with them and getting to know their needs as a group and as individuals, the worker forms a positive relationship and helps them to engage in socially acceptable activities which they come to choose. The basic goal is helping them to change undesirable attitudes and patterns of behavior. (p. 21)

The detached youthworker programs in New York City, Los Angeles, Boston, and Chicago received the most attention in the literature, although there are references to programs in San Francisco (e.g., Bernstein, 1964), Philadelphia (e.g., Philadelphia, PA, Department of Welfare, 1963; Bernstein, 1964), Los Angeles (e.g., Waltz, 1946; Los Angeles County, CA, Probation Department, 1965), Detroit (e.g., Bernstein, 1964), and Cleveland (e.g., Welfare Federation of Cleveland, 1959; Bernstein, 1964). Tables 1 and 2 summarize these programs in terms of underlying assumptions (Table 1) and program goals (Table 2).

TABLE 1. Underlying Assumptions

CHICAGO AREA:

1. Delinquency is principally a product of the breakdown of the machinery of spontaneous social control.

2. Delinquency is seen as adaptive behavior on the part of male children of rural migrants acting as members of adolescent peer groups in their efforts to find their way to meaningful and respected adult roles essentially unaided by the older generation and under the influence of criminal models for whom the inner city areas furnish a haven.

3. The aims of a juvenile delinquency program must be embraced by the local population.

4. Residents of high delinquency areas must take action themselves. Delinquency areas must be utilized to take leadership roles in any delinquency programs.

NEW YORK CITY:

1. The success of the project depends largely on the personalities, skills, and techniques of the workers.

2. The workers must have the capacity to understand and deeply appreciate the communities in which the gangs live and operate.

3. Understanding of individual and group behavior, skills in group work and recreation, and a high degree of flexibility in their attitude.

4. Involves the application of sound, generic social work principles.

5. Participation in a street gang is seen as natural and as part of the growing up process of adolescence, and the group has the potential for promoting positive growth.

6. Patterns of anti-social behavior are a result of external factors in the environment or in the family.

7. Repressive measures may be necessary for the protection of the community but do not change basic attitudes or behavior.

8. Street gang members can be reached and will respond to sympathy, acceptance, affection, and understanding when approached by adults who possess these characteristics and reach out to them on their own level.

9. The relationship developed between the worker and a street club can serve as a catalytic agent for modifying anti-social attitudes and behavior and can help the individual member meet his needs in positive ways.

10. To be effective the program must be coordinated, unified, and applied on a saturation basis.

11. Because of the relationship developed between the worker and the group it is imperative that the worker be assigned to only one group.

BOSTON-SPECIAL PROGRAMS:

1. The phenomenon of the "corner crowd" is a natural positive factor that can be used.

2. Belief that a positive relationship with the gang members can be established by an adult.

3. Accept the members without accepting their behavior.

4. Belief that these adolescents are not satisfied with their situation and will move toward more satisfying and more acceptable behavior if they are given enough help and support from an understanding adult and if this is done within the framework of the hanging crowd that is of such vital significance.

5. Worker is a substitute for a "good parent."

6. Need to accept the group at its current level of interest and activity before attempting to help it to change.

TABLE 2. Goals of Detached Youthwork Programs

CHICAGO AREA PROJECT:

1. Reduction of juvenile delinquent acts.

2. Foster the development of knowledge and competence in the conduct of youth welfare activities and encourage among residents of high delinquency areas confidence in their own capacities to act with respect to their problems.

3. Provide opportunities for the community to change its values, and as a result the youth will change theirs.

NEW YORK CITY YOUTH BOARD:

1. Provide a series of real experiences for the group that might result in changes in their general world-view, as well as in the standards by which they judge their own behavior and that of their friends.

2. Reduce gang fighting.

3. Control delinquent behavior.

4. Rehabilitate the group.

5. Provide access to opportunities.

6. Change values.

7. Prevent further delinquency.

8. Responsible for self-direction.

9. Improved community relations.

Three Model Programs

Chicago, Los Angeles, and New York

The three programs reviewed here are examples of city-wide, "saturation" programs run by independent agencies in cooperation with local governments and voluntary agencies. The *Chicago Area Project,* established in 1934, was based on the theories of Shaw (see, e.g., Shaw & Jacobs, 1940) and employed indigenous workers.

The *Los Angeles Youth Project,* founded in 1945, was designed by social service executives and academic juvenile delinquency experts. It was unique in that community agencies came together voluntarily and grappled with difficult issues, ostensibly without engaging in "turf battles." Their first recommendation was the establishment of a Special Service Unit to develop programs for delinquent youth gangs and to work with agencies in developing such programs. To accomplish this, individuals were hired by the project to work directly with youth on the streets. No title was given to these workers; their task was to "go out to the streets" and somehow engage the "unadjusted" youth, to "work with them," and then to bring the group into two existing social agencies and other programs.

The *New York City Youth Board* initially used existing agencies as a starting point for detached worker programs but removed all except one after 18 months because:

> There were wide variations in the application of the method: some used the worker as a recruiter for the agency; others worked with unaffiliated social rather than anti-social groups; one agency which was affiliated with a public law enforcing program encountered conflict between the detached worker and the gang. (New York City Youth Board, 1952, p. 101)

The detached workers were placed under the auspices of the Youth Board, and later caseworkers and community organizers were included as part of a team approach. Thus, recognition was given to the concern for both individual and community issues and the interrelationships among them.

As is shown in Table 1, the underlying assumptions of the three programs were quite similar, with the Chicago Area Project being the most adamant in its belief that the entire community must be involved in changing behavior and attitudes. This is also reflected in the program goals in Table 2.

Basic Requirements. Bernstein (1964) believed that individual agencies could successfully use the detached youthworker method if the following elements were present: First, there must be financial stability; second, there should be a firm and vital commitment to lower class youth;[2] third, the agency must possess imagination, flexibility, and integrity; and last, the agency must be ready to move in whatever direction the problems require, with an honest readiness to examine failures (p. 65). The Youth Board in New York City also acknowledged that an individual agency could take on such programs

> . . . providing the agency has an accepting, "reaching-out" attitude toward these hard-to-reach groups and has adequate staff, both quantitatively and qualitatively, to cope with the situation. (New York City Youth Board, 1952)

Did These Programs Work?

Testimonials. The literature is filled with many claims and testimonials about the effectiveness of detached youthwork (e.g., Bernstein, 1964; New York City Youth Board, 1952, 1960, 1965; Caplan et al., 1963; Freeman, 1956; Kobrin, 1959; Dumpson, 1949; Ackely & Fliegel, 1960; Juvenile Delinquency Evaluation Project, 1960).

From these studies a major theme emerges about program effectiveness: The most dramatic changes occur in public group behavior (e.g., thefts, vandalism, fighting); second, in public individual behavior; and the least dramatic changes occur in private individual behavior (drinking, gambling, sex, etc.). Bernstein (1964) believed that changes in private behavior were almost always linked to other changes (e.g., job, school, identification with the worker). Other measures of change noted include staying in or returning to school, involvement in organized activities of other agencies, referrals to other professionals, obtaining and keeping jobs, taking more responsibility for one's own actions, better relations with the community, better health care; and a more positive attitude toward the future in terms of perceptions of one's ability to affect it.

Telling examples of the importance of the detached youthworker to the youth are the several incidents noted in Bernstein's (1964) study where unserved groups "acted-out" in dramatic fashion to secure the attention and services of a worker (p. 27).

Formal studies. Although there were no large scale empirical studies of detached youthwork, there were a few studies of individual programs. For example, Miller (1959) found in Boston that law-violating acts by delinquent gang members had been substantially reduced, with a net decline of 25%. He related this to the efforts of the detached youthworkers. Two other indicators of success he used included a decrease in commitments to correctional institutions and the fact that age groups in vertical, integrated gangs became more separated. Positive results were correlated to the amount of time the detached worker spent with the group. Yet he later reported (Miller, 1962) that there was no significant change in law-violating or morally-disapproved behavior. He did, however, find changes in other forms of behavior (e.g., structural changes in groups, etc.).

Grandy's (1959) evaluation of the Chicago Hyde Park Youth Project found that 46% of the gang members were less involved in anti-social behavior (with 22% showing no anti-social activities at the beginning or at the end of the evaluation). The percentage of positive change among the more socially deviant was even sharper. These changes, too, were attributed in part to the work of the detached youthworkers. It is important to note that none of the studies reviewed concluded that detached youthwork was sufficient by itself to either control or prevent delinquent gang behavior (e.g., New York Board, 1965), while all agreed that such work was necessary.

METHODS/TECHNIQUES/PROCESSES OF DETACHED YOUTHWORK

The title—whether "detached youthwork," "corner work," "area work," "extension work," "street gang work," etc.—describes the position and some of the activities of a worker. Clearly, the major technique, method, process or even, as some say, the theory of detached youthwork (e.g., New York City Youth Board, 1965) or the philosophy (e.g., Freeman, 1956) involves "going to where the youth are," be it the street corner, the corner store, pool hall, alley, or park. Associated with this notion is the primacy of the relationship between the youth and the worker. From these two concepts all of youthwork flows. The New York City Youth Board (1952) summarized it this way:

> Detached youthwork starts with a problem, not a program, and its heart is the individual worker and the basic tool is his personal relationship to his group; much of the content of his approach is substantially determined by the nature of the problem he faces. (p. 49)

Reaching Out

"Being on the street" can be looked at as a process, a method, or a philosophy. The process of street work is best seen through the eyes of a detached youthworker, the methods through the profession of social work, and the philosophy through academic sociology. Hanson (1964) quoted a detached youthworker's description of the process:

> To hang around and become part of the neighborhood in which the gang hangs out (usually the toughest, most deprived, most dangerous areas of the city) . . . to get to know and become friendly with the gang members (who are the most suspicious kids alive, hostile to strangers and distrustful to all adults) . . . with affection, acceptance, and understanding, to try to re-direct their energies into less destructive, more socially acceptable channels. (p. 8)

And the thoughts of another worker on the process of "reaching out":

> It takes patience, a few minor miracles, and an inexhaustible supply of faith, hope, and love. And endurance. All the faith, the hope, the love, all the psychology, common sense, and compassion depended, in the long run, on sheer physical endurance . . . walking, talking, and walking and talking. (p. 109)

From a social work perspective, the methods used in the initial phase of reaching out are described in a series of specific steps, a set of social work principles or, in the case of Spergel (1962), as a multidimensional model of practice. Austin (1957) lists a series of steps a detached youthworker should anticipate: First, an initial period of exploration in the community; second, a first verbal contact with the members of a specific gang or group; third, a period of intense testing by the group; fourth, establishment of a contract through which the worker will have continued contact with them; and fifth, movement into an extended period of mutual interaction during which the most significant activity of the worker takes place.

A list of principles to be used in this "reaching out" phase can be found in a number of articles (e.g., New York City Youth Board, 1962). These include: A service that starts with a problem, not a program; a service that is made available at the point of greatest need rather than at the point where those most eager for a program have paid a fee, etc.; an understanding of the neighborhood and acknowledgement of the group's frame of reference; meeting the group at its current level of interest and activity before attempting to help it to decide to change; accepting or being as nonjudgmental as much as possible about the behavior; and enhancing self-esteem by giving support and by introducing ego-building activities leading to group success.

Freeman (1956) described the philosophy of detached youthwork as a series of beliefs: First, the "corner crowd" is a "natural" formation and there are many positive aspects of it that can be strengthened by a worker; second, a relationship can be established by an adult; third, one can accept the youth without accepting the behavior; and fourth, that delinquent teenagers are not satisfied with their situation and will move toward more satisfying and more acceptable behavior if they are given enough help and support from an understanding adult, and if this is done within the framework of the "crowd" which is of such vital significance to them.

In 1965, the New York City Youth Board explicitly stated its theory of street work as follows:

> ... street work is the result of an interaction between the individual worker and the street gang; although the worker comes to his task with a certain set of goals and values he wishes to communicate to the group, his techniques are considerably determined by the nature of the problems he meets. (p. 58)

Establishing the Relationship

The establishment of a relationship between the worker and the youth can be considered as a social process or a series of interconnected steps. A quote from a new youthworker working with a gang of girls exemplifies this sense of process (Hanson, 1964):

> You try to remember what you really believe, that the noise and the bravado and selfishness hide a hungry child. Hungry for love, for attention, for respect and decency–and all too often, for food. You will teach and preach, instruct and persuade . . . a youthworker's voice can get very tired. Then one day she'll decide you're for real. You don't have an angle and you're not a kook. She doesn't understand it, but she accepts . . . you'll begin to see the signs. . . . It doesn't always happen that way, of course. Not eight times out of ten, or even five times out of ten. But it happens. And when it does, you'll know that even if it happens only one time out of a hundred, it's enough . . . until the next time, it's enough. (p. 21)

Bernstein (1964) described the establishment of the relationship as a central dynamic for change,

> . . . as a well-spring of potentially health-giving waters flowing toward a better future. It requires dedication, patience, skill, a feeling for the teenagers and the harsh realities within which they live, and a sense of fun with the ability to share in their legitimate pleasures. It opens new vistas of trust, activities, and community concern and resources. (p. 88)

The establishment of the relationship can also be described in terms of discrete activities (New York City Youth Board, 1952):

> Hanging around, making small talk, establishing contact . . . involving much testing and re-testing. (p. 108)

Young people's confidence in the worker came more through specific, concrete actions–e.g., helping them get jobs, coaching teams, passing around cigarettes (then more acceptable than now), paying for pool, visiting boys in jail, etc.–than through any verbal statements. Bernstein (1964) described the stages as recognition, contact, association, influence, and help with specific problems. Freeman (1956) described the establishment of the relationship as one that starts with being a "referee," moves to being a "diverter," and then moves to being an "exhorter." Clearly, the worker-youth relationship is basic and crucial.

Evolution of the Relationship

In his analysis of the content records of a group of workers, Freeman (1956) found that explicit goals were rarely mentioned, there was a marked progression on the worker's part from more passive to more active activity, "testing behavior" occurred in all phases, and "attention-getting" activity, after an initially high rate, dropped off and fluctuated irregularly at a lower level. Ego-strengthening activities grew steadily with time, and conscience-building activity began late and showed a rather steady increase. Assistance in expression of feelings and limitation of dependency occurred in clusters, showing no general trends over time, but was related to individual or group crises.

He found that both group ego-building and activity to minimize conflict existed at a rather steady rate from early in the record, while the fostering of extra-group relations built up more slowly but leveled off at a steady rate after the fifth month. Group conscience-building also reached a plateau after the fifth month. Group effectiveness picked up after the fifth month and sustained itself at a steady rate. Overall, he found that as the relationship between the worker and the youth deepened, the role of the worker moved steadily toward one of being a change agent.[3]

Freeman (1956) described the relationship as:

> A substitute for a "good parent," i.e., one who is not overly controlling but who can recognize and begin to fill dependency needs–once those needs are satisfied, (the youth) will feel stronger and make further attempts to achieve independence . . . this is the theoretical justification for the worker's being an exceptionally giving person . . . serving also as a role model. (p. 17)

Bernstein (1964) also found that the worker taking on some of the role of parent was a critical part of the relationship. Yet the New York City Youth Board (1965) found that only 9% of the youth saw the worker in the role of a parent.

Activities

The day-to-day activities of individual detached youthworkers varied greatly and were most significant in the context of the relationship. Such activities ranged from giving a haircut (Bernstein, 1964) to intensive counseling of an acutely suicidal youth (Hanson, 1964). The New York City Youth Board (1965) summarized the activities of youthworkers as:

> Tasks which are "never finished" . . . where all of the ground rules cannot be laid out in advance. The tasks must be seen as a continuing process in which the worker confronts a group of youth whose behavior changes from week to week. By his mere presence on the street, the worker is a powerful stimulant to the creation, maintenance, or dissolution of the group itself. As the group changes, so also many the worker's objective for service change. It is more than conceivable that as different styles of deviant behavior emerge, the worker will be confronting a group whose needs for service may be quite different from those for which the project was originally formulated. (p. 12)

Here is seen the early recognition of street youthwork as emergent, evolving, and (almost) never-ending.

A number of studies have analyzed youthworker activities. The most simplistic categorization is from a social work perspective: a youthworker does casework, group work, and community organization or, as Freeman (1956) called it in the language of that day, "generic social work." Others, such as Spergel (1962), argued that the task of youthworkers could be viewed as multidimensional and categorized as:

(1) Sociocultural: Activities that modify institutional arrangements blocking opportunities for youth and facilite the provision of opportunities by the official representatives of key institutions;
(2) Small group activities that enable the group to meet the collective needs of its members for status (not friendship or sociability) and which modify group process, member orientation, and behavior; and
(3) Discrete activities that are therapeutic in nature and focus on how the individual youth reacts to acceptance or rejection, frustration or stress, and security or insecurity, and on what his or her

seemingly enduring patterns of personality and relationships are (pp. 65-68). Within this context also are activities that involve direct intervention in the network of significant interpersonal relationships of the youth.

In the early years of detached youthwork there were significant differences between the activities of female detached youthworkers (usually working with girls) and male youthworkers (usually working with boys). The goal of altering the values and the behavior of the youth was similar, but the values and behaviors that were the focus for change and the specific activities used were quite different for the boys and the girls. Activities with girls were oriented toward

> transforming the girls from Sex Objects into Good Wives by introducing them to the finer points of makeup, hair styling, cooking, dressmaking, and etiquette . . . (Campbell, 1984, p. 16)

while the goal with boys was to just stop them from fighting.

YOUTHWORKERS

Despite the fact that virtually all studies discussed the importance of the relationship between the worker and the gang and often explicitly cited it as the critical element in the success of the detached youthwork method, none was found that took the youth's perspective, and only six examined detached youthwork from the perspective of the youthworker (Bernstein, 1964; Caplan et al., 1963; Freeman, 1956; Hanson, 1964; New York City Youth Board, 1965). This section examines who the workers were, their career patterns, their goal aspirations, their motivations, and their personal frustrations, as well as the critical issues of supervision and training.

Who Are the Detached Youthworkers?

An overview of all studies about youthwork suggests that most youthworkers were male and were divided almost equally between African-Americans and Caucasians. (The first program to use women was the Special Youth Program in Boston in 1954.) Most people began this work in their twenties, and they brought a wide range of backgrounds and training to the field. For example, the Chicago Area

Project used residents of high delinquency areas under the tutelage of staff sociologists, while the early programs in New York City hired individuals who had been trained in recreation, physical education, teaching, psychology, anthropology, and social psychology. It appears that two of the early programs, the Los Angeles Project and the Special Youth Program in Boston used only social workers with master's degrees.

Workers in later programs (Bernstein, 1964) also had a wide variety of educational backgrounds, with most having a baccalaureate degree. Bernstein also noted that the workers had a wide variety of interests and skills and a great deal of practical knowledge (e.g., giving haircuts, fixing cars, etc.).

The social backgrounds of the workers were varied as well. For example, in its study of 111 youthworkers, the New York City Youth Board (1965) found that 47.5% had grown up in large cities, 27.5% in small towns, and 23.8% in other urban environments; only one had grown up in a rural community. Over sixty percent of the workers came from neighborhoods similar to the ones in which they worked; 40% of all youthworkers reported that they had had the same or similar adolescent group experiences. The Board noted that these findings were virtually identical to the statistics in the early 1950s, when there were fewer workers and the project was much less extensive (p. 45). Bernstein (1964) found that the majority of workers said that they had had adolescent experiences similar to those of the youth with whom they worked.

Worker Qualities

In hiring and describing workers, programs focused on personal characteristics rather than academic qualifications. The literature is filled with adjectives describing the qualities necessary to do detached youthwork. Among the most common are, "a desire to help," "independent," "dedicated," "abundant energy," "empathy," "courage," "flexibility," "sense of fun," "inventiveness," "ability to think on one's feet," "honest," "firm standards of morality," "self-understanding," "good common sense," "patience," and "faith" (e.g., Austin, 1957; Bernstein, 1964, Freeman, 1956; New York City Youth Board, 1952, 1965).

Motives

The overwhelming majority (80%) of the workers in the New York Project chose this field because of a desire "to help youngsters" and "to try to reduce delinquency."[4] This was true also in Bernstein's (1964) study:

> It would be an abuse of psychiatric insight to attempt to claim that these large number of workers are primarily motivated by needs to control, to work out problems hanging over from their own youth or by other kinds of underground mechanisms. Purity is rare in these matters, but the primacy of the desire to help is true of the great majority of street workers, and it was heart-warming to feel its reflection in talking with them. (p. 111)

The New York Youth Board's (1965) study of workers also commented upon this commitment of the workers:

> [the] honesty, integrity, and selflessness of the majority of street workers were remarkable. (p. vi)

Workers' View of Their Work

The New York Youth Board (1965) described the worker's own role definition as follows:

> By becoming readily available and accessible in times of crisis and general social need, the worker can build significant relationships with his group and be accessible for help. (pp. 52-53)

The workers in Bernstein's (1964) study corroborated this definition in their belief that the greatest strength of the detached youthwork model lay in the opportunities created by having a trusted and resourceful professional present and available to the youth when needed or wanted by them (p. 96). When asked which role description most aptly characterized their work, thirty percent of the New York City Youth Board's (1965) participants responded that their main responsibility was to help with an individual's "social needs," while 30.8% saw themselves functioning primarily as group workers, 13.3% saw themselves primarily as individual counselors, and 13.3% as social service agents "on call."

Eighty-five percent of the workers in the New York study agreed that the goal of street work

> . . . is to help the group members channel their behavior and values into more constructive forms of expression so that these youngsters might become contributing members of the community. (p. 66)

Specific goals mentioned included prevention of gang fighting, securing employment, making individual referrals to social service agencies, meeting with neighborhood organizations, and counseling the group and individual members about home, school, or neighborhood problems.

The group services mentioned most frequently in this study were "hanging around" and planned recreational activities and trips; the most frequently mentioned individual services included locating job opportunities, family visiting, and individual counseling. The workers also saw acting as a change agent for the community or neighborhood in which they worked as a large part of their job. A common experience of many of the workers was that they would "step into whatever vacuum appeared in the area" (p. 55). The Board expressed concern that the longer the workers remained in the area, the more the community expected of them and, in turn, the more problems the workers accepted as part of their responsibilities (p. 67). One worker described it this way:

> I have a feeling the worker is getting swallowed up in his own attempts to do his job precisely because the demands made on him span such an unrealistically large number of social needs. (p. 55)

In the New York City Youth Board (1965) study, the overwhelming majority of workers believed that the youth saw them as "professional youthworkers," 7.7% of the workers believed that the youths' initial perception was one of confusion about their role, 9.5% thought the youth saw them as a "cop," and two of the workers believed that the youths' initial perception of the detached youthworker was as being "one of the boys."

Several authors were concerned about the isolation of the detached youthworker, in the sense of being "alone on the street" in relation to what was expected of them. For example, Spergel (1966) stated:

> The streetworker stands alone on the street corner in the provision of his service. Fewer supports of routine supervision and administrative

structure are available to him than to almost any other type of social agency worker. A great deal of knowledge, skill, independence, and sheer courage are required of the worker in the exercise of his role. (p. 52)

Yet the Youth Board study found that more than half of the workers believed that they were able to solicit help and direction easily. About a third felt that they were their own best resource person, and only 16.7% felt in general that they were alone on the job. Bernstein (1964) also found that most of the workers did not express a sense of isolation.

View of Agency

Youthworkers frequently viewed their agencies as obstacles to their work with youth (Bernstein, 1964; New York City Youth Board, 1965). Their most frequent complaints included the political nature of the agency, the "red tape," too much paperwork, and a feeling on the part of many workers that the agencies devoted resources to needs less acute than those of street youth. The Board acknowledged the political constraints in its 1965 report, noting that it

> ... is a political agency whose best interests might well be served by continuing to function in approved ways, which often means what is politically feasible rather than what might be a more adventuresome attempt to meet the changing demands of its delinquent groups. (p. 11)

The great majority of workers in the 1965 New York Youth Board study were satisfied with the communication between themselves and their direct supervisors, while only 67% were satisfied with the communication between themselves and the agency's central administration. Length of service was negatively correlated with the degree of satisfaction between the worker and both the agency and the supervisor; satisfaction tended to decrease the longer the worker had been there.

Training

Two studies looked at whether and how detached youthworkers were trained. Bernstein (1964) stated that the curricula of schools of social work most closely match the needs of the detached youthworker. He commented, however, that the training of most youthworkers was far from what was needed:

> . . . we face the disturbing gap between the need for the highest levels and enormous ranges of skills and workers who begin with little beyond general education and perhaps a good life experience. (p. 116)

Workers mentioned that more training was needed on working with and understanding individual and family dynamics, psychopathology (even in those agencies that downplayed this), group work, understanding the politics and interactions between social welfare institutions and the community, and appropriate subcultures. The majority of the workers in the 1965 Youth Board study complained that the training they had received was too theoretical and not realistic or practical enough. The same was found true in the Bernstein (1964) study:

> When [youthworkers are] brought together for training, there are tendencies toward impatience with generalized theory and professional lingo and an eagerness for applications to situations which trouble them . . . the trainer needs to know their problems, to understand their language, and [to] be ready for their aggression. If he is successful in breaking through, he reaches the dedicated, thoughtful and eager-to-learn person so many of them are. (p. 115)

Supervision

The New York City Youth Board (1956, 1960, 1962) consistently emphasized the importance of supervision. Early in the development of its detached youthworker program, the Board developed a structured supervisory process. It included having each worker develop a general statement of his or her philosophical outlook on delinquency and the methods that he or she felt would be most effective in coping with it. The purpose of this was to "fix and locate certain established and fundamental values" (p. 148). Supervisors also had new workers verbalize what they experienced on "the street," while continuously pushing for clarification. Additionally, the Board encouraged regular group meetings of workers as a way to "process" their work.

Career Patterns

Only Bernstein (1964) and the New York City Youth Board (1960) addressed the issue of career patterns, both acknowledging that recruitment was easy but the turnover rate was high. Bernstein believed that "burnout" and lack of opportunity for advancement were the critical factors in the turnover rate. He also noted that many of the workers talked of the change in lifestyle required to do the job (essentially being on call 24 hours a day) and the havoc that the job created in marriage and family relationships. While Bernstein did not attribute the turnover rate to this factor, it seems likely that it played a role (and continues to do so).

Profession or Subculture?

Bernstein (1964) viewed detached youthwork as a subculture with a slogan of "always for the underdog," describing it as having:

> A strong, almost fierce dedication to the youth and their problems, with little patience for the society and the community institutions which seem to neglect them . . . a scorn for the 9 to 5'ers, which even extended to staffs of their own agencies, who were regarded as too middle-class . . . some impatience for service to more conforming youth and other segments of the populations and a feeling that their agencies were devoting resources to needs far less acute than those of the sub-lower-class youth. (p. 113)

The existence of such a subculture is given credence when one reads process notes of workers (e.g., New York City Youth Board, 1960) or when reading Hanson's (1964) description of the life of a female youthworker:

> Gradually and irresistibly, she was drawn into the barrio, sucked into its atmosphere, its mores, its attitudes, and its fears. Her speech took on a Spanish flavor, nearly incomprehensible with the gang slang and sudden halts to edit out the four-letter words which had become familiar to her ears. She grew restless away from the area; she ate, slept, dreamed, and talked about "her girls." (p. 14)

In this subculture is found three recurring themes: The tightropes that detached youthworkers must walk; the lack of professional identification; and the low status, poor pay, and short career ladder.

The tightrope walked by detached youthworkers is not only between the youth and police, but also between the youth and the sponsoring agency. For example, Bernstein (1964) says,

> He is rooted in two worlds and a balance between them is not easily attained . . . . (p. 113)

Hanson (1964) quotes a youthworker as follows:

> You've got to walk a tightrope. You can't be a stool pigeon and you can't be a patsy, and there isn't any formula to go by . . . these kids have to learn that you can be their friend and still stand for law and order, too. (pp. 51-52)

The New York City Youth Board (1962) states that there are many tensions between worker and agency that stem from the autonomy of workers and the decentralization of their functions, professional "touchiness" arising between departments, and pressure of workers to maintain some distance from the administration in order to remain free to control the activities most crucially concerned with their work (p. 10).

With the exception of the Chicago Area Project, all agencies viewed the job of detached youthworker as professional in nature, yet none called it a profession of youthwork, nor did they place it clearly and explicitly within the social work profession. For example, in its policy manual, the New York City Youth Board (1949) states that "Streetwork is a professional community service" (p. 43). Spergel (1962) argues for a multidimensional model for social work practice and uses detached youthwork as an example of such practice, but he never states that detached youthworkers are social workers. Freeman (1956) looked at the job of youthwork as "generic social work" (p. 9), i.e., doing group and casework at the same time, but did not call the detached workers social workers.

The New York City Youth Board (1965) suggested that the central problem of professionalism was that the workers do, to a great extent, the work of professionally trained social workers and yet are not identified, or trained as part of the social work profession. This threatens the professionally trained social workers and creates turf issues (p. 76).

Caplan et al. (1963) comment on the lack of identification of youthwork with a clear body of knowledge, noting that it is

. . . evident that despite training and experience, the common conceptual framework applied by the workers studied, with the exception of one worker, appears to be built largely upon a series of common sense expectations that would apply to almost any interpersonal relationships . . . their conception of interpersonal relations is not yet systematic and rationalized . . . share many of the role characteristics of teachers, foremen, or policemen; their roles do not yet have a technical vocabulary and a corresponding set of practices that would distinguish them from such informal roles as parent, friend, neighbor. (p. 7)

This lack of professional orientation contributes to the third recurring theme: Lack of status, low pay and a short career ladder. Bernstein (1964) summarizes this succinctly stating that

. . . all too many of these workers regard themselves as composing the staff of an agency but not clearly part of a profession. In addition to missing the stimulation, support, and fellowship which being identified with a profession provides, they lose the sense of a life-long commitment, of going somewhere. The present job is transitional. (p. 116)

A uniform finding in the New York City Youth Board's (1995) study of youthworkers was the general dissatisfaction among workers about their status and pay. One worker summed it up this way:

Streetwork is not dignified; workers receive an annual income that is far short of a living wage, especially when you judge it in terms of the hours of time the job demands and when these hours occur . . . (p. 75)

But youthworkers in this study also felt that they were often "talked down to"; not involved in making policy decisions but simply informed of them and told to "make them work"; and treated by other professionals as workers who lack professional standing (i.e., whose job it is simply to pave the way for more highly trained caseworkers and community organization consultants):

With the average youthworker seen as . . . something of a maverick (i.e., needing excitement, having a sense of restlessness, and treasuring a high degree of autonomy and independence). (Bernstein, 1964, p. 112)

and with the lack of professional identification, the low status, the low pay, and the development of a subculture, the detached youthworker is placed in a role within his or her agency analogous to that of the role of a gang member with respect to the larger society. Bernstein's comment about the status of agencies often reflecting the status of the people they serve also appears to apply to the status of detached youthworkers within those agencies.

SUMMARY

Even a cursory familiarity with current streetwork and street youthworkers is enough to enable one to recognize in this historical overview patterns and language that are contemporary, indeed sound like the very voices heard in this study. This continuity in structure, pattern, and voice may follow from the fact that the structure of the work then and now is remarkably similar. Soon we will learn whether the workers, too, are like their historical elders.

NOTES

1. The knowledgeable insider could locate the use of each of these terms in time, space, and academic source, for each is shorthand for a complex of philosophy, program, and worker. However, these distinctions are not important here.

2. There is the danger that the streetwork program will come to be given the same marginal status as is accorded to the minority and lower-class people it primarily serves.

3. This may simply reflect a standardized rhetorical presentation in the record of how the worker does youthwork, e.g., how he or she does records (Garfinkel, 1967; Tice, 1998).

4. These kinds of responses could be read as workers "being workers," i.e., as trying to "look good" and/or as "wiseguys" playing with the researcher.

Chapter III

Methodology– How Did We Do It?

SELECTION OF A RESEARCH MODEL

... at the time of its inception, psychology was unique in the extent to which its institutionalization preceded its content and its method preceded its problems. (Koch, 1959, p. 738)

That method was the empirical model and even today, mainstream American psychology continues to accept the validity of the positivist empirical model and often sees it as the only model (e.g., Colaizzi, 1978; May, 1960). Yet, as Siegal (1977) suggests, methodology is very much like theory:

It is a way of illuminating and interrelating selected aspects or components .... (p. 80)

Thus, the methodology one chooses greatly affects what is seen, what is thought to be important, and the ways in which findings are interpreted, presented, and used. It is with this in mind that I explored a number of possible approaches appropriate to the research question.

The question, "What is detached youthwork and how is it practiced?" is directed at understanding human beings and "being human" within a given context–that of detached youthwork. The phenomenological approach was selected partly because it is a research method that attempts entry into the "conceptual world" (Geertz,

[Haworth co-indexing entry note]: "Methodology–How Did We Do It?" Thompson, Jacquelyn Kay. Co-published simultaneously in *Child & Youth Services* (The Haworth Press, Inc.) Vol. 19, No. 2, 1999, pp. 35-42; and: *Caring on the Streets: A Study of Detached Youthworkers* (Jacquelyn Kay Thompson) The Haworth Press, Inc., 1999, pp. 35-42. Single or multiple copies of this article are available for a fee from The Haworth Document Delivery Service [1-800-342-9678, 9:00 a.m. - 5:00 p.m. (EST). E-mail address: getinfo@haworthpressinc.com].

35

1979) of a group and attempts to understand what their experiences mean to the participants. One can, then, order and integrate these meanings into a model that reflects both the common sense, everyday understanding of the phenomena and the larger understandings of social science. The findings can then have a number of uses, ranging from direct planning on a very practical level to providing deeper understanding of the studied phenomena on a more abstract level (Siegal, 1977, p. 80).

The phenomenological approach was selected for several other reasons as well. First, while there is extensive literature on detached youthwork and it has been described, "measured," and "analyzed," no studies were found that attempted to understand this occupation from within the "conceptual world" of the detached youthworker– even though the major theme found in this literature is the primacy of the detached youthworkers' relationship to the youth with whom they work.

Second, having worked in the field for seventeen years both as a detached youthworker and more recently as a supervisor of detached youthworkers, I had become painfully aware of the great discrepancy between what is said by youthworkers publicly and what they experience and talk about privately to each other. This method is a way of tapping into the "private world" of youthworkers through dialogue in an atmosphere of trust, where individuals are not reduced to "subjects" and used only as sources of data. Rather, the phenomenological interview allows interaction with the "whole person," and the research situation itself becomes a "lived situation."

Third, the phenomenological method is rooted in description (Colaizzi, 1970, p. 5), acknowledges the "irreducibility of experience," and looks for meanings within the context of those experiences, thus reducing the tendency to develop analytic or explanatory constructs prematurely. It allows for the presentation of the situation, the way a situation is, and the way in which it is lived, experienced, and reflected by the participants. It is also an approach used to find the essentials:

> the description of those invariant constitutes which are not universal nor particular, but general. (Wertz, 1983, p. 50)

Finally, this is a way of "being in the world" with which I am comfortable and about which I am knowledgeable, and one that is not seen as "intrusive" by the youthworkers themselves.

Limitations of the Approach

There are limitations both in the approach and, as a result, in this individual study. While the model is one that is "intuitively" understood by many in the youthwork profession (via many personal communications with detached youthworkers), it often appears to be "soft," "non-scientific," or "biased" to administrators of such programs (via personal communications with administrators) and to many in mainstream psychology (e.g., see Giorgi, 1985). Thus, these findings may seem trivial to and be dismissed by some significant individuals and groups.

A second limitation in this kind of research is the skill of the researcher, because the procedure demands heightened self-awareness, willingness to confront one's presuppositions, and the ability to connect with and listen to another person and to hear what he or she is saying.

There are ways to confront and respond to these potential limitations. As with all research methods, one must use and document them in rigorous and systematic ways so that others can assess the work. One can also present "findings" as partial, tentative, and temporary, and thus resist claiming "truth" when only one perspective was documented; i.e., not oversell the study. Third, this method can be incorporated into studies using other methods, thus allowing for data comparison, and the method can be used in the sense of an early, descriptive approach.

Specifically, the limitations of this study include the fact that there may have been too many subjects; a smaller number would have allowed for more in-depth searching with each. It might have been more useful to have interviewed all the people involved in one detached youthwork program (e.g., administrators, supervisors, etc.), thus providing a more complete picture of the context in which detached workers do their work, rather than covering several less intensively. Third, a random sample was not used. Instead, the interviews involved volunteers from the youthwork community in one metropolitan area. Thus, in a positivistic sense, the findings have low generalizability. Last, having worked in the field and in the same metropolitan area for the past seventeen years, I brought into the interview my reputation, my association with an agency, and the everyday reality of agency and city politics.

It is not known how these factors may have inhibited, constrained, or otherwise influenced the interviews. As a check on this, a colleague interviewed two of the participants. My understanding of detached youth-work also made it easy for me to believe that I "intuitively" understood what I thought the individuals were saying. This I countered by con-sciously, conscientiously, and consistently asking each person to "clari-fy," "further explain," or "talk in greater detail about" their experiences so that my "taken-for-granted" understanding would be held in check, thus allowing their understandings to emerge.

RESEARCH PROCEDURE

While the tools of phenomenological psychological research vary and are not yet available in a "cookbook," there are a number of essential features to this approach (Bogdan & Biklen, 1982): First, the natural setting is used as the direct source of data; second, the re-searcher is a key player in the research; third, it is descriptive and concerned with the process of the study as well as the "outcomes" or "products"; fourth, such research is more inductive than deductive, so the direction of the study may emerge after the data has been col-lected; and last, personal meaning is an essential concern.

The method used in this study attempted to be faithful to these essen-tial features. The natural setting is the youthworker as a person. I, the researcher, bring my own presuppositions to the study, and I am aware of and explicit about them. This is a descriptive study that uses as its basic data the actual words of the youthworkers and their understandings of the topic being discussed. Data collection was by personal interviews that were transcribed verbatim. How the youthworkers interpret and what sense they make of experiences–i.e., what it means to be a youthworker and how one who is a youthworker does everyday work and non-work life–became research foci. Last, the data drove the analyses. Thus, an inductive method was used to analyze data and "grounded theory" was developed. Abstractions were built from particulars. Both were the sub-ject and substance of the psychological reflective method.

> Part of the very meaning of phenomenology is not to seize upon a particular method and impose it everywhere but rather to develop appropriate methods precisely in contact with each unique phe-nomenon. (Wertz, 1985, p. 160)

To do this, a number of different ways of approaching phenomena were examined (e.g., Colaizzi, 1973, 1975; Giorgi, 1975, 1985; May, 1960; Wertz, 1985) and the following procedure was developed.

Procedural Outline

1. My biases and presuppositions were made explicit so that if another researcher "assumed the same attitude," he or she could perceive and understand the same meanings–not necessarily to agree, but be able to understand and explicitly state what the disagreement was about. To accomplish, this I reviewed my own writings about youthwork, reflected on my beliefs, hypotheses, attitudes, and hunches about detached youthwork, listened to myself talk with others about the study, asked friends, peers, and supervisors what they heard me saying about detached youthwork, and used all these sources of data to prepare an *individual phenomenological statement.*

2. A focus group of five youthworkers met for five sessions, each approximately three hours in length. The time was unstructured and the only question asked was, "What is detached youthwork?" The sessions were taped and transcribed.

3. A second group of twelve youthworkers met for twelve weekly three-hour sessions; the questions asked included:
   A. What is detached youthwork and who defines it?
   B. What is a good youthworker and who defines this?
   C. What do you need to do, to do youthwork?
   D. What does it mean to be a youthworker?

   Notes taken during the twelve weeks were organized and typed.

4. A structured individual interview form was developed using the data obtained from these two initial groups (see Appendix A).

5. Approval for the use of human subjects was obtained from the University of Minnesota Human Subjects Committee to enable faculty at the University to use the raw data.

6. The following criterion was used to identify youthworkers eligible to participate in the study: "Agency affiliated, with primary responsibility to work with youth in the community." Seventeen detached youthworkers working in the St. Paul-Minneapolis

metropolitan area were then recruited through a non-random sampling procedure using word-of-mouth contacts in the local "youthwork community" and an announcement at a large public meeting of youthworkers.

Each person who agreed to be interviewed was informed of the purpose of the interview, was asked to sign a "Consent Form" (see Appendix B), and was told that a copy of the completed study would be made available to them. Interviews were conducted in a variety of settings, such as individuals' offices, their homes and in restaurants, lasting for an average of four hours. Each person was interviewed using the structured interview, and the interviews were taped and transcribed. All identifying data were removed during the transcription (see Appendix C for a sample interview).

7. Relevatory description. Each detached youthworker interview was read twice, with the intent of "grasping the meanings expressed as the speaker intended" (Michael Baizerman, personal communication, 1990).

8. Demarcation of meaning units. Meaning units (i.e., a group of words reflecting a particular meaning) were identified within each interview. They were grouped to form "contextual themes." "Horizontal themes" (i.e., themes across interviews) were developed by grouping contextual themes (i.e., themes within each interview). These themes reflected the structure (what) and the style (how) of detached youthwork.

9. Each interview was reproduced on a different colored paper and meaning units were cut out and sorted into themes. They were then attached to large cardboard sheets, each sheet reflecting one horizontal theme.

10. After all meaning units had been sorted and clusters of meaning units constructed, the themes were compared to the original interviews to enhance their validity and reliability. To facilitate this, the following questions were asked:

   A. Is there anything in the original interviews that is not accounted for in the clusters of themes?

    B. Do the clusters of themes suggest anything that is not stated or implied in the original interviews?

    Discrepancies found between and/or among the various clusters were noted and accepted, since "what is logically inexplicable may be existentially real and valid" (Giorgi, 1970, p. 17).

11. All comments made by the researcher within the interviews were read and meaning units were developed, clustered into themes, and attached to cardboard sheets, with each sheet reflecting a theme.[5] These were then referred back to the investigator's individual phenomenological statement (#1 above) to insure that all were accounted for.

12. The themes were reviewed and reflected upon from the perspective of phenomenological psychology. This step was both a "discovery" and a "creation," a moving from objects to their meaning. The result was another kind or level of understanding of the meaning of youthwork.

13. Three core themes emerged from the longer list: *Becoming* a youthworker; *Doing* youthwork; and *Being* a youthworker. All of the smaller themes were regrouped into one of these three larger ones.

14. The experiences of "becoming" a youthworker, "doing" youthwork, and "being" a youthworker, as given in the interviews, were reviewed and reflected upon on two levels, the individual and the class of "youthworkers." From these reflections and from the use of "imaginative variation" (i.e., looking at what else it *could* be), a "specified realm of generality" (Wertz, 1985, p. 191) was created and visually represented as the essence of youthwork and how it is lived and practiced.

15. The interviews completed by a colleague were examined for similarities and differences and then included as a part of the study.

16. All results were shared with three previously-interviewed detached youthworkers, to deepen further the analyses.

SUMMARY

These sixteen steps constituted the research procedure, which was designed to implement a phenomenological psychological approach grounded in theory and method. Applied herein, these steps enabled the study to derive the phenomenological essence of detached youthwork, as is seen in the following chapter.

NOTE

5. See Appendix D for a list of the seventeen themes that emerged from the data. Appendix E provides an example of the components of one such theme, "The Youthwork Stance."

Chapter IV

Results–
What Do We Know?

This chapter is divided into four sections: A description of those interviewed; an individual phenomenological statement of my biases and my attitude in approaching this study; the results of the data analysis in terms of the *becoming, doing,* and *being* of detached youthwork, and a pictorial description of the essence of detached youthwork and how it is practiced.

DEMOGRAPHIC DESCRIPTION

Seventeen detached youthworkers in the Minneapolis-St. Paul area were interviewed, fifteen by the author and two by a colleague. The latter two interviews showed no differences in the amount or in the type of data collected.

The age, sex, education, current job, employment history, and past experiences in the field of detached youthwork were the demographic variables on which data were collected, to help put the workers' experiences and the meanings of these experiences into context.

Of the 17 workers interviewed, 14 (82%) were Caucasian and the other three were African-American. Nine (53%) were female and the age range of the group was from 26 to 42 years, with an average age of 32.2 years.

Fourteen (82%) had baccalaureate degrees and four had completed at least one year of graduate school. The remaining three had completed at least two years of college. The majority had attended private

[Haworth co-indexing entry note]: "Results–What Do We Know?" Thompson, Jacquelyn Kay. Co-published simultaneously in *Child & Youth Services* (The Haworth Press, Inc.) Vol. 19, No. 2, 1999, pp. 43-68; and: *Caring on the Streets: A Study of Detached Youthworkers* (Jacquelyn Kay Thompson) The Haworth Press, Inc., 1999, pp. 43-68. Single or multiple copies of this article are available for a fee from The Haworth Document Delivery Service [1-800-342-9678, 9:00 a.m. - 5:00 p.m. (EST). E-mail address: getinfo@haworthpressinc.com].

43

colleges and had majored in a variety of subjects including education, nursing, social work, psychology, fine arts, and criminal justice. Five (29%) had bachelor degrees in social work. The majority of those interviewed had spent most of their career working with youth (mean = 8.2 years), with an average of 3.4 years in detached youthwork (the range was 1 to 10 years). They had held an average of 2.3 jobs each. A pattern of moving from more structured, rigid working environments (e.g., a residential treatment center) to less structured, more fluid working environments (e.g., detached youthwork) was noted for 13 (76%) of those interviewed.

INDIVIDUAL PHENOMENOLOGICAL STATEMENT (OR, I WEAR TENNIS SHOES, TOO)

About ten years ago, I attended the funeral of a client who was sixteen years old. She had been involved in prostitution and had been murdered. Below is an excerpt from my journal, written shortly after the funeral:

> I sat in the church on the left hand side. I was sitting with a group of "professionals"–teachers from her school, social workers who had worked with her family, probation officers, police officers and me, a youthworker. We sat in this church, listening to the Southern Black Baptist minister stumble around for the right words to say. I noticed the different kinds of people who were all seated in this one room. Up toward the front of the church were her parents, brother, and two sisters. Behind them were her grandparents, aunts, and uncles. To the right were her school friends. Behind them were friends from her church youth group. Then to the left were us–the helping professionals. Way in the back of the church (they came in after the service had started) were five young women about her age who had "worked the streets" with her. As I looked around, it was clear to me that this young woman had been many different things to many different people. She was someone's daughter, sister, granddaughter, niece, friend, student, client, colleague, and "hooker."

All of these people–of different ages, sexes, and colors, were crying. Maybe we cried for the same reason, maybe for different reasons. But we all felt some sense of loss. As the service ended, I walked up to the casket and said, "May you have peace on your journey." This I said for me. I watched as the casket was carried out of the church and placed in the hearse. The people followed behind. It was at this moment that I realized what youthwork is (at least in part). As people started talking with one another, I found myself introducing the professionals to the family, the friends to each other and to the family. It became clear that I was the only one there who knew everyone else. I knew her family. I knew the professionals. I knew the friends from school, from church, and from the streets. I knew and could weave in and out of her many worlds. I knew her as someone else's daughter, as a sister, granddaughter, student, friend, and "hooker." And as a youthworker, all of these aspects of her created my "client" and created me as a "youthworker."

There are many other beliefs, thoughts, and hypotheses about what youthwork is and how it is practiced in my journals, in hastily written notes to myself, and in articles and grant proposals that I have written. Unfortunately, my thoughts, observations, insights, and knowledge do not seem to follow a natural pattern, to flow smoothly. Instead, my understanding seems to come together for a moment, then–poof–it is gone. Then it comes together again, but now in a different way. The following thoughts are themes in my understanding of youthwork, themes because they are ideas that persist:

• Youthwork as a function, not as a status
• Youthwork as a verb, not as a noun
• Youthwork as a process, not as a task
• Youthwork as an art
• Youthwork as a moral statement
• Youthwork as teacher and student
• Youthwork as a profession
• Youthwork as a way of "doing life"

I acknowledge these as part of my own understanding of my "attitude" as I approached this study. Yet one cannot be totally detached from what one knows (Giorgi, 1975), nor can one know fully what one knows until life invites it to show itself. To be aware and explicit about my own "taken-for-grantedness" was to use these to inform and not to sabotage; to heighten my sensitivity to the others' own struggles to understand and to the meanings they produced; to realize that to the extent I can know myself, I can hear them teach me who they are.

Interviewing became "talking," occasionally "dialogue." This was little different than "working with a kid," only harder!

There is also much that I do not know about me and about youthwork, and much that I question, struggle with, and am conflicted about. All of these also affected how I approached this study and thus it is essential to make them explicit.

I have wondered about my past, my biography, how I have come to be as I am. There have been times when I have been intensely involved in understanding and evaluating my past. At such times, I have usually been in, or close to being in, therapy—reconstructing, analyzing, and making sense of me in the context of another.

These last few months have served as such a time. When I decided to do this study, I was very conscious that it was going to be a self-exploration in the context of studying others. What I did not anticipate was the depth of that exploration, the issues that it would raise for me, the questions that would be left unanswered, the thoughts and feelings it would evoke. I have flipped from experiencing myself as a very cheap "whore" who has been used by police, by youth agencies, by kids, and by families, to experiencing myself as being one of the last of the '60s diehards: A rebel without a cause!

I have found in my old writings issues I have not yet resolved, questions I have not yet answered. For example: "If I compromise, am I selling out? Does compromise change who you are? Is awareness and understanding sufficient, or must I act on these—even when I'm not sure or am exhausted? When I realize that I experience a moral conflict, how do I struggle with and resolve it? What is integrity? What is success for me? If I am successful, have I sacrificed personal relationships or clients, and does that act within itself lack integrity? Have I ever betrayed a client to "the system"?

I come back to these thoughts, questions, and issues now, after 17 years in the field of detached youthwork, as I struggle to find some meaning in, attach some meaning to, or wrench some meaning from those years. As Colaizzi (1978) said:

> All human research, particularly psychological research, is a mode of existential therapy. (p. 69)

This is what this project has become for me—a struggle for meaning and understanding. Equally important, it is an attempt to define what I

am becoming (a way of *becoming, doing,* and *being*). For me, in a psychoanalytical sense, the study is a transitional object.
One of my professors told this story:

> There was a man sitting on the bank of a river when he saw a woman drowning. He immediately jumped into the river and dragged her to safety. Having saved her life, he had no more than sat back down when he saw a man in the middle of the river screaming for help. He again jumped up and swam to the man's rescue. After getting the man to safety he turned to see that there were now two more people in the river drowning. This kept up for quite a while, with the man dragging one person after another to safety. Being very tired, he thought that maybe he should go up the river to see who was throwing these people in and tell them to stop.
>
> Once the man saw the bigger picture, i.e., a pattern–someone or something throwing people into the river–he asked himself: "What is the right thing to do? What is the right way to do it? If I go up the river to check on what is going on–who will save the ones already in the river? What if I go up the river and find more than one reason for people ending up in the river? What if no one listens to me? What if they throw me in?"

Like the man at the river bank, detached youthworkers struggle every day with such issues and choices. When one works with youth who are homeless, abused, chemically dependent, pregnant, "doing prostitution," and/or who have AIDS, the question of doing the "right" thing in the "right" way becomes a daily dilemma, e.g., do you take money from the Playboy Foundation to "save" females who are involved in prostitution? The right thing seems to be to "save" these kids, yet is money from such a source the right way? Or is the right thing to "save prostitutes," like the man at the river tried to do, whatever the means?

I have, maybe, "saved" 700 to 800 kids during my seventeen years doing youthwork. My guess would be that at least that many have turned to the streets in any *one* year. Did I focus at the right place? The need to deal with the "urgent" (the "drowning kid") versus the "important" (the underlying social causes) causes me great anguish. Often I have tried to do both. But I did not "solve" the problem. So, am I a part of the cause of that or related problems? I do not believe that these questions (and others like them) have final answers. Rather, such questions are more like a checklist to keep me honest. But I can never be sure that my own answers are complete. I must ask others what they experience. Thus, this study is dialogical, my entering into questions and answers within myself and with others—my colleagues, friends, and "alter-egos." This is an attempt to do no more or less than to "meet with the other," who is sometimes myself.

BECOMING A DETACHED YOUTHWORKER

There are many paths to becoming a detached youthworker. The social career is unclear; the pathways to, through, and out of this occupation are unique to each individual, as are the time and the trajectory. There is no prescribed coursework, training program, or college degree; no licenses to obtain, tests to be passed, or professional organizations certifying one as a detached youthworker. This section examines, from the youthworker's point of view, how the participants came to be detached youthworkers.

Early Personal History

The youthworkers gave many explanations for how they came to this kind of work. Some were personal, in the sense of wanting to give to others what they had received as children or wanting to provide what they had not had as children:

> I chose to work with kids just because of what happened to me when I was young and I didn't get the help that I wish I would have got back then . . .

> . . . some of it for me, too, is growing up. When I was a teenager it's like I wanted somebody in my life that was going to sort of guide me because I was having a whole lot of trouble figuring out, kind of, where to go and what to do, things like that. It was always like in the back of my head that I wanted to work, if I ever survived that period, I wanted to work with kids because it was so yucky for me.

Several workers mentioned specific people who had helped and influenced them while they were adolescents; for some, it was an adult mentor. To each, it was the meaning of these relationships that, in retrospect, was a source of interest in this work and later a reason for becoming a detached youthworker:

> . . . my Dad has been a role model in that he's just a real caring person. Within our neighborhood he was always wanting or will-ing to help people out and go out of his way . . . .

> . . . because I always thought that I was off the wall.

> I liked to travel and I liked to read. And my family's telling me to do this kind of thing, that kind of thing. She was the one person, this little 65-year-old nun, saying: "No, you're right. It's okay to do that stuff and that's something you're always going to have and that's something to be treasured." . . . she liked who I was and she found a lot of value . . . in my kind of social deviance. She saw that stuff as strength and always labeled it as strength, like cross-dressing as an adolescent, and she got it. And she thought it was hysterical because I was working–I was working so hard to go, "Oh well, f--- you . . . I'm not one of your kids. F--- you, I'm somebody else." And she appreciated that. And she was also always like gut-honest with me. I would go in and I would say, "I think this is really f---ed." And she'd say, "Yep, you're right. This is f---ed."

Three individuals knew from an early age that working with people was what they wanted to do, yet, none had set out to be a youthworker. For example:

> I remember in second grade is when I decided I was going to be in human services. Social work was all I knew, so I decided I would be a social worker.

Later Sources

Self-Understanding

A number of the group admitted that detached youthwork was a means they chose to understand themselves:

. . . Oh God . . . I've made such leaps and bounds and again I think one of my purposes of even going in this profession–. . . and I don't know if I've thought about this directly or consciously–was to figure my own self out and try to work out some of those issues that weren't worked out in adolescence.

. . . but it seems like what has driven me in the work is that it is tied to me understanding myself. . . .

Classes

One person moved into the field after taking a youth studies course:

I set out to be an artist and quite accidently I took a youth studies course. By the second class I was–oh, this stuff is cool, I could do this. I was really bitten by it then. There was something they were doing that was really different from what I thought psychology was.

Praxis

For others, becoming a detached youthworker was a way to live out their beliefs:

It's a life. I can say it is a lifestyle. It is the way . . . I look at life. I think it is more of an approach to society's problems. I guess what I do fits within my philosophy of life–the job lets me be me.

The world is pretty f---ed up. We need to do something about it. The best way is to start with the kids.

. . . doing this is leading to a better, more civilized adult population twenty years down the road. . . .

Emergence on the Job

Most of the group entered detached youthwork after working in more restrictive environments; that did not provide the freedom to do what they felt was "right":

I started out working in a residential treatment center, but it really wasn't *working* with kids, it was maintaining the status quo. . . .

Then I started doing some family work . . . then I just moved to working with the kids. . . .

. . . I always wanted to teach . . . but it was too restrictive and structured. . . . The lack of structure in what I do now gives me the chance to be creative and do things that I like.

Learning the Job

School Is Not the Answer

Where does one learn to be a detached youthworker? Formal education does not seem to be the answer. No one in the study thought that formal education was of particular importance in becoming a youthworker:

I don't think that youthworkers need technical information. They don't need to be taught step by step procedures.

What Is Needed Is a Mentor

What *is* needed, according to many of those interviewed, is a mentor, a person who challenges them, makes them think through issues, forces them to look at things in a different way, and yet values and trusts them as good human beings:

. . . she just taught me a great deal because she was extremely frank and blunt. I remember I'd sit there and complain: "I can't believe these kids . . . I can't believe what kind of place they are in . . . they are doing this . . . they are doing that. . . . " She said, "Well, what are you doing?" She pointed out things that I was doing that contributed to the situation that I was complaining about. So it really made me look at what I bring to the situation, what I bring to relationships. . . . She was a mentor-type person.

. . . I got a lot of individual attention and feedback

. . . Just learning a lot of those things about boundaries, about separating what's my issue from what the caller's issue is and all those kinds of things. . . . He constantly challenged me. . . .

... the most effective mentor and the greatest learning that I got came from people who related to me on a personal level. It wasn't somebody saying, "This is what it is and you need to learn it." ... it was a constant personal relationship and personal dialogue which made me think, which brought out feelings and made me deal with all kinds of stuff. I think that is something that probably doesn't happen when somebody's dictating, "This is what needs to happen."

The Self as Teacher

Youthworkers say that to learn this job, one must have the ability to think through events and experiences, to observe one's self and others, to explore and expand one's self, and to see "becoming" as an ongoing process:

... I learn best by watching, by listening, by observing myself and others in given situations. . . .

... it is a never-ending process of making sense out of what is, what isn't, and what could be. . . .

... it's an evolution. . . .

Other Sources

Feedback from the youth, trial and error, and calling upon one's own experiences as an adolescent are other major ways in which one learns to become a detached youthworker:

... It was trial and error. . . . This feels right and that doesn't. . . .

... feedback from the kids. They let you know what is valuable and what is not.

... I draw heavily on my experiences as a youth. I think I draw on it a lot.

... in thinking about this interview today, one of the things that I thought about was that as a kid we used to get the police to chase us. This was exciting for us. And we could always ditch them.

They could never catch us when we got into yards and go between the houses. . . . One night, there was a new cop on the force and when we ran around behind this house he was standing there and saying, "Where are you going, boys?". . . . and when I thought about that, I thought about youthwork and how I think sometimes being out in front of youth, so when they come around a corner you're already there, that you understand, you understand where they were going and perhaps why they were going. . . . And that is something that comes directly from my experiences as a young person.

Summary

Entry into detached youthwork is through many doors, some deliberately chosen as a way to live a life consistent with one's beliefs and values or as a way to give others what one received or did not receive as an adolescent. For other youthworkers, the door was a serendipitous one–a door that opened because of a particular person, experience, or event–while for still others it was a natural progression of working with youth, a movement from structured, rigid environments to less structured, freer ones that, often with the help of a mentor, allowed the worker to use his or her talents in more creative and "real" ways. Or some combination of the above.

Unlike entry into most jobs, entry into detached youthwork is a life process, not a series of formal procedures. There are no degrees to pursue, tests to pass, or credentials to get. The process of "becoming" continues through the act of "doing."

DOING DETACHED YOUTHWORK

Although all those interviewed were called "detached youthworker," "detached streetworker," or "detached social worker," none was doing "traditional" detached youthwork in the sense of being on the street working with gangs (e.g., New York City Youth Board, 1952, 1960, 1965), as was described in Chapter I. Yet all were more or less detached from their agencies in their work.

"Detached" from What?

According to the youthworkers, "being on the streets" was seen by all but one of the agencies primarily as a way of increasing their client populations rather than being of value in and of itself, as it was viewed in major metropolitan areas in the late 1940s through the early 1960s (e.g., New York City Youth Board, 1962), as was shown in Chapter I:

> To the agency it means that you spend X hours on the "street" . . . scheduled times . . . finding kids and telling them about the center.

Who Do They Work With?

The detached streetworker programs of the late 1940s through the early 1960s focused primarily on working with a group of youth (i.e., a gang) in a particular neighborhood. The traditional detached streetworker did work with individuals, but this was secondary to the goals of preventing delinquent acts and resocializing gang members toward more "traditional" values and beliefs. Youthworkers today focus on "unaffiliated" youth, and the vast majority of time is spent with individual youth and families in population groups of youth who have been labeled by others as having a particular "problem" (e.g., AIDS, gay or lesbian, etc.). For example:

> . . . kids who are misunderstood.

> . . . these kids don't fit.

> . . . a kid who is troubled. . . . Something's wrong in their lives; either their family is screwed up or they have a drug problem, they have been abused, or someone who is really struggling with what is going on.

Working Conditions

As were traditional detached youthworkers, these workers were on 24-hour call, received the lowest pay of human service professionals within their agencies, and often had the largest "case loads":

> We work the most hours, get the lowest pay, see the most kids, and get no respect.

> We're treated just like our kids. . . . We work the hardest, the longest, and yet are not seen as professionals.

Our wages are not even living wages and yet it's impossible to get a part-time job because we're on 24-hour call.

Work Activities

The activities of these youthworkers ranged from educational to providing "therapy," as well as others:

> . . . say a kid can't come to pre-natal class, or they have a kid that's particularly, what you call a street kid, or somebody that's not as easy to get into the clinic, I may go out to where they are and do education pieces . . . .

> . . . I'm finding that I'm doing therapy with kids, which I've never really done before. I'm doing a lot more individual stuff with boys who are victims of sexual and physical abuse. . . .

Other activities mentioned by workers include advocacy, crisis counseling, driving kids to and from places, playing with them, helping them take care of daily tasks (homework, keeping appointments, child care, etc.), helping them find a "passion" in life, politicizing them, and helping them to "fight" smarter.

Supervision

Supervision of detached youthworkers was consistently mentioned in the literature as a key element in worker satisfaction and program success (e.g., Bernstein, 1964; New York City Youth Board; 1965). From the perspective of these detached youthworkers, there was essentially no effective supervision. To them, supervisors lacked an understanding of what workers do, they were unavailable when needed, and they did not provide the support the workers needed to be effective. For example:

> . . . administrators always think we're going to be able to do five million things and the kids think that, too, so it gets pretty overwhelming at times.

> . . . it is like we are hired and cut loose—we are very detached!

Supervision? Within my agency, I don't feel like I have one. We're on our own. We can do what we want to do.

... they (administration) put in more rules, greater structure, and more paperwork and then become less accessible.

The majority of those interviewed talked about wanting and needing supervision–supervision that is safe, i.e., where one can really talk about what is going on with the kids, with oneself, and in the community without fear of overreaction, "lectures," or more bureaucractic red tape. The workers talked of needing support, someone who understands what they do and why they do it, feedback, insulation from the bureaucracy, and an advocate for themselves and their clients within the larger bureaucracies. They also want supervisors to be teachers who can connect theory to practice and practice to theory. They also want them to be mentors in the sense of role models who ask tough questions and help them interpret and translate bureaucratic issues and "politics."

Working with Youth

Developing Relationships

The youthworkers were clear about what they perceived as their goals for working with youth: Primarily to develop relationships with them and then to help them with whatever both see as needing to be done. One person saw the relationship as an end in itself:

> I meet kids and I form relationships with them, and with a lot of them for no other reason than that they're there.

A variety of ways of developing relationships with youth were mentioned by the workers: "Just being there and hanging around," providing advocacy, making available a variety of resources, going on outings, coaching athletic teams, leading support and "therapy" groups, "playing," and "counseling." These are similar to the traditional methods used by street youthworkers working with gangs.

Most of the interviewees saw the purpose of the worker-youth relationship as being a way in which they could come to know an individual youth as a human being, understand her or his world from that perspective and, in so doing, "affirm" (Friedman, 1983) him or her. Many of the workers also saw the relationship as one that provided a way of letting the youth figure out a better way to "do life," and to be more satisfied or happy:

. . . worked really hard at trying to understand the world the way kids understood it, not the way adults did, which is part of learning how to listen and hear what they need . . . .

. . . giving a kid permission to go after his dreams . . . providing the resources, the support, or whatever is needed to move toward what will make him happy or satisfied.

While the traditional detached streetworker saw the need to change youth behavior and attitudes so as to fit the broader social culture as a primary goal, the youthworker today sees the goal as helping the youth to "find" his or her own values, style, and way of "doing life"–whether or not these fit into the broader social culture:

. . . I think it has to be somebody who helps you with whatever brings meaning to your life and allows you to do that. . . .

. . . I think there needs to be a movement with kids, not this puppet stuff, and if there is a group of skilled professionals who are giving the support, they can pave the way politically and systems-wise to let these kids do that . . . and restructure the whole educational system. . . .

. . . can affirm the kid for his differences, and really allow the kid to own and be proud of his differences and . . . let the kids explore who they are and develop that with a minimum of constraints and outside shaping.

Work at the Interface: Being a Translator

Doing youthwork also means serving as a translator between youth and parents, youth and school, youth and traditional social service agencies, between and among professionals, and between the youth and the world at large. This means that the youthworker must learn the language of many different groups and professions:

. . . translating what the kid says to the parent, teacher, social service agency, or judge . . . or from the social worker to the psychologist. Each profession seems to have its own language and we, the youthworkers, are the group that seems to understand and speak them all. . . .

Conception of the Job

Youthworkers tend to hold a core set of values, attitudes, and beliefs that appear, according to those interviewed, to be essential as means to establish positive, helping relationships. These are consistent with those of traditional detached youthworkers, yet the current detached youthworkers are clearly working toward different goals for themselves. It is this congruence to past worker beliefs and styles that makes the youthworkers of today seem like they share a common belief system, even a similar subculture, with traditional detached youthworkers. All of them said that to do youthwork, one has to see "worth" in the adolescent where others do not see such value and must genuinely respect and care about these youth as *human* beings. Critical also are an "attitude of openness," a desire to understand youth as they exist in their world and as they see themselves in that world, and an acceptance of youth as who they are and "where they are at":

> . . . a decided fondness for young people. . . .

> . . . working with kids, dealing with kids, playing with kids, or whatever, you have to first of all value where they are, what they are, and who they are. . . .

> . . . worked really hard at trying to understand the world the way kids understand it, not the way adults do.

> . . . have to be as close to nonjudgmental as they (detached youthworkers) can. . . .

> . . . nonjudgmental. . . .

> . . . I think in youthwork you meet kids from all sorts of situations. You can't be judgmental about what's going on in their lives. . . .

Another common belief is "hope" but, as one youthworker aptly put it, it is hopefulness without rose-colored glasses:

> . . . it's being a very twisted kind of person, (one) who can . . . always expect and suspect the worst, at the same time not believing it, knowing that there is hope.

There is said to be a youthwork "mind set," a "stance" of youthwork, of "doing" youthwork. The key elements of this include acknowledgment that the youth sets the direction of the worker-youth relationship, and that the worker must focus on "what is," the now, the gritty reality, and the context in which it occurs. The latter is necessary because it provides a partial understanding of the youth's experiences and what they mean to him or her. Finally, since the worker cannot be everything to every youth, one must act as a broker of services:

> . . . works with kids from the perspective that the kid directs what happens. . . . The kid is in charge. You don't go in with an agenda of problems or solutions. . . .

> I think it comes back to two things. (First) I think part of it comes back to the whole idea that we can't define it, we can't name it, and we don't have a cause-effect and conclusion. (Second) we can't deal with it because our society is so sequential; this needs to lead to this and that needs to lead to that, and here's the response.

> What I do is less formal; it's more kid-oriented in that the kid writes the agenda with me. The social workers within this agency are very time-oriented, kids have to come to them, but I can go to the kids. . . .

> There is no meaning without an understanding of the context in which things occur. . . .

> We act as a resource, . . . knowing where things might be, how to get them, . . . and ways around the system.

> I find safe places within the system for kids. . . . I know the "good" psychologists, the "right" school, the "best" probation officer.

Summary

Doing detached youthwork involves more than the activities listed on a job description, which themselves vary greatly from simple acts, such as giving a ride to a kid who needs to go to the doctor, to complex and intense community organization activities. Activities cannot stand alone but must be viewed within the context in which they occur. "Doing" detached youthwork always involves "being" a youthworker.

BEING A DETACHED YOUTHWORKER

The "doing" of detached youthwork and the "being" of detached youthworkers are seen as inextricably intertwined. Detached youthwork puts philosophy into action; it is a praxis. It is a matter of "where you stand," not your specific methodology. It is a form of being human with another human being; one does not "practice a profession," use techniques, or systematically apply a given scientific theory to a given situation. One acts and lives a philosophy of "caring-in-action." This is a summary, in my words, of the participants' sense of what being a detached youthworker means.

I never heard them use the phrase *"practicing* detached streetwork." Rather, what was said in the interviews and what can be gleaned from field notes of traditional detached streetworkers (e.g., New York City Youth Board, 1952) is that it is in "the context of *being* that *doing* occurs. Thus, what is done may not be as important as who does it, or what and who one is. This tension between and among personal authenticity, youth needs, and job requirements is basic to the "being" of a detached youthworker.

Is Youthwork a Profession?

One definition of profession (Gould et al., 1964) is:

> Occupations which demand a highly specialized knowledge and skill acquired at least in part by courses of a more or less theoretical nature and not by practice alone, tested by some form of examination either at a university or some other authorized institution, and conveying to the persons who possess them considerable authority in relation to "clients." (p. 542)

Using this definition, detached youthwork is not a profession (nor is it a semi-profession, Etzioni, 1969). While there is specialized knowledge–a *craft* knowledge (Bensman & Lilienfeld, 1973)–involved in the work, there is not a base of highly specialized knowledge nor is there (yet) any examination that one can take to be accredited or certified as a detached youthworker. Yet detached youthworkers do possess considerable informal and sometimes formal authority in relation to their "clients." Thus, they do have responsibility, but they lack the concomitant external recognition and validation. This discrepancy causes much ambivalence for the workers.

Lack of Acknowledgment

Over and over again, the lack of acknowledgement from other professionals, from family and friends, and even from one another contributes to their ambivalence about the professionalism of the field and to their own sense of self as professionals. When one adds to this ambivalence the low pay, the infrequent interaction between the worker and other agency staff, and the often infrequent contact with workers from other youth agencies, it becomes clear that the ambivalence has social sources that are reflected in worker self-image and feelings:

> . . . if you are working with kids you are just working with kids, and people say, "Well, it's not a profession." I really thought it was until I started working with some of the systems stuff, and I don't know that it is viewed as a profession. My grandmother keeps calling me and saying, "Well, someday, if you stay with your company long enough, you'll get a better job. You won't have to be outside so much and you won't have to work with those kids; you'll get to work with 'real' people." In some weird kind of way I think she represents a lot of people.

> . . . such a non-value to so many people. I can't go home and explain to my family what I do and get validation for it. I get condescending responses but I never get really good stuff . . . people don't get what I do. Even when people sit and really want to know and really listen and really hear me, they don't get what I do. And that goes back to my stuff about working with no validation and needing people to understand what I do and why I do it. But at the same time I think that there's something inherent in the field, that it's just not valued.

> I think it can be a profession. I don't think it's perceived as that . . . [it] makes sense that you call youthwork [a profession] because it seems to be a way of working, of being in the world that is there. It's just not very recognized.

> . . . I think youthwork takes a certain kind of person . . . it's a specialty . . . it's a knowledge about working with people that I don't think everybody has and I don't think everybody or just anybody can do it.

Ambivalence About Youthwork as a Profession

Youthworkers are also ambivalent about whether detached youth-work *should* be a profession because of the negative images that they appear to evoke among other helping professionals. Concerns raised about youthwork being (or becoming) a profession include becoming "turf"-oriented (i.e., fighting over which kid "belongs" to whom), using established rules and practices as a way of justifying one's behavior rather than having to take responsibility for what you do and don't do, compromising in action so as to protect one's status, and the use of credentials as the only way of deciding who is qualified:

> Oh, God. There are times when I want to say, "yes." But then I look at other professions and all the stuff that's f---ed up about having to be a profession and I don't want it to be a profession.

The relevance of these comments is highlighted when one looks at the formal definitions of profession:

> Such authority is carefully maintained and often deliberately height-ened by guild-like associations of the practitioners which lay down rules of entry, training, and behavior in relation to the public (pro-fessional ethics), see to it that the standard of knowledge and skill of the practitioners is not lowered, defend the level of their profession-al remuneration, try to prevent competing groups from encroaching upon the boundaries of their professional activities, and watch over the preservation of their professional status. (Gould et al., p. 542)

Youthwork as a Calling

A broader definition of profession can be found (Onions, 1933, p. 1593), one that uses the word *calling*, defined as: "A strong inner impulse toward a particular course of action or duty" (p. 549). The majority of interviewees spoke of youthwork as a calling.[6] It is from this perspective that, although they may see their work as a profession on a cognitive level, many detached youthworkers do not experience themselves as professionals.

> . . . it is what I need to do. . . .

I get charged by dealing with someone who has a pierced nose. I don't know, it's stupid stuff, but it's a calling and if I'm not doing it, I get nuts. The times when I haven't done very much youthwork, and done more school, I start to feel pretty meaningless.

If I'm not doing youthwork, I'm bored.

There are a lot of times I wish I didn't know what I know. Then I wouldn't feel so compelled, so driven, whatever, to do something about it.

But you have to have a vision of some sort. . . . I couldn't continue to do this kind of work if I didn't think I was making a difference with any kid; I wouldn't do it. I don't know where the whole notion of trying to help people comes from but it's just something I have always had. . . .

I call myself a professional, but that's on an intellectual level. On a gut level, I don't feel like a professional. I think that it is based on the way society looks at what we do–what *I* do. And what other people think I do.

Youthwork as a Lifestyle

All the detached youthworkers understood their work as a commitment to a lifestyle more than to a job or a profession. This is the "being" of a detached youthworker. This lifestyle includes being available 24 hours a day, living "on the edge," a way of looking at the world whether or not you are working, and an inability on the part of others to discern when one is working or not working:

> . . . if someone was following me around all day long or even following me around for a week, I think it would be hard for them to figure out when I was working and when I wasn't. . . . The way I do life is the way I do work.

> . . . while I'm not working, I'm working. . . . I go to my sister's for Christmas and worry about what my kids are doing, do they have anything for Christmas? I get mad at my nieces because they get presents and I ask why–why do these kids deserve these presents and the kids on the street don't?

. . . but they also had something to do with youthwork too, because both of those people were youthworkers and it was kind of what their life was about. It wasn't just their job, it was sort of the way their life worked.

Values

Also, part of the youthwork frame is a set of values about "the self" in the context of being a detached youthworker: The need to be comfortable with oneself, to be honest with oneself, and to look continually at oneself were mentioned by every youthworker. This "need" reflects the core belief that "Who you are is what you do":

Youthwork has you look at you. It's like, I genuinely have to consistently look at where I am and what the f--- I'm doing, you know. Which is why I don't think people stay in youthwork very long, because you come to a point when you realize you've come back to that painful adolescence or [even] beyond.

Morality and Ethics

Here is seen the anti-technocratic ideology as a source of job strain, the lack of an identified code of ethics, the need to be "genuine and real," and a belief in the value of youth. The ability to acknowledge one's responsibility to the agency and to the larger community means that being a youthworker involves a constant struggle about what is right (and for whom). It means paying attention to one's own actions, talking with colleagues, looking at the larger picture, and always being "grounded" to the morality of a situation.

More important, this says that morality and ethics are everyday, mundane aspects of practice, not abstract codes or rules. This is so for people with little or no education in ethics and morality, with little or no supervision, and with little or no opportunity to talk with colleagues about such matters. Thus, morality and ethics become elements of the detached youthwork philosophy-in-use and reflective philosophy (Schon, 1983), and often the worker becomes a "super-ego" for agencies and the larger community. This has the potential to create strain between the worker and the agency:

. . . Yeah, it's an interpretive process in that I think the youth-worker probably listens to what the kid says and then . . . accepts that as their reality and says based on that standard that this is good or bad or helpful or not helpful. I think the thing that winds up being different for youthworkers is that they seem to be more subjective, so that I could see a situation where . . . in one setting with a kid, a particular action is seen as ethical, good, right, whatever, and in another situation with another kid it would be not right or whatever.

So it changes all the time, whereas social worker and psychs seem to me to want to more often have a consistency. They want to talk about norms, they want to talk about statistical averages and how close people they come to what it seems like everybody else does. Most youthworkers don't place much stock in that; they go with each individual kid each time and kind of figure that out as they go along. So it's not uncommon to me to hear youthworkers talk about, "I feel like I'm flying by the seat of my pants." There's a sense of, I don't know what's right here or what's wrong; I have to figure it out each time. Whereas more often I'll hear psychologists or social workers talking about averages, about norms, about aggregates.

. . . so it's like a kid that you're supposed to refer or a kid that you're supposed to turn into the f---ing immigration or something like that, or call the police on, you know you're supposed to do that, and it would be easier to do that because then you don't have to sit with this kid. . . .

Yeah, and I know this because I know what social work is. The difference is that social work is a thing of seeing people within the context of their system. The problem of social work as a profession is that it's completely sold out to money so that you continually betray your clients to the system by getting them into the system that you already know is f---ed. I mean that's the difference. A youthworker won't do that. A youthworker won't do that without saying, "I'm putting you into the system right now but it's f---ed and here's 'a,' 'b,' 'c'–don't get caught into that."

Thus, detached youthworkers struggle with some of the same issues as the youth with whom they work–feelings of being oppressed, of not being valued, of being alienated and alone–and with issues of control and anger:

... I think one of my problems was that I didn't have enough confidence in my intuitive sense about what was going on–to tell her, "No." And I'm not saying that's all it would take, but I think part of it has to be youthworkers themselves starting to see themselves in a more positive way. I think it's tempting for a youthworker, and I think this happens a lot, because it's happened to me anyway, to align myself with my clients. And to see myself as an oppressed person. I think I communicate that when I communicate with other professions, when I defer to another professional. When I don't see myself as a powerful professional, in a powerful position, because I'm connected with the kid.

Being a detached youthworker also means "going up against the system," "living on the fringes," and, oftentimes, feeling as if one is constantly "on the edge":

... as much as you find yourself fighting or wanting to fight or wanting to be able to quit fighting the system. . . . A lot of times you feel like the system really works in a way opposite of what you'd like to see happen for a kid. . . . . You go up against it and you advocate for them within that system and you fight for them and then you try to have a kid understand the system and you try to work around it or within it, or whichever way. It might work, but I guess in that sense I feel somewhat on the fringes. . . .

... you'd have to be a revolutionary in this society because if you're focused on social justice, you would have to be immediately aware that this is an unjust society and your mission, then, in actuality, would not be to work with people but help fight the unjust system.

Summary

To the detached youthworker, *being* a detached youthworker means living in a way that is "real," "authentic," and filled with paradoxes and moral dilemmas. It involves a complex set of values, beliefs, and attitudes that come into play not only during the working day (or night), but in all parts of one's life at all times. Being a detached youthworker means focusing on one's relationships with youth, with agencies, with the larger community, and with oneself. It is a questioning and an understanding of "what is," a hope for "what could be," and a lot of action aimed at moving from "what is" to "what could be."

FIGURE 1. What Is Youthwork? (It Depends)

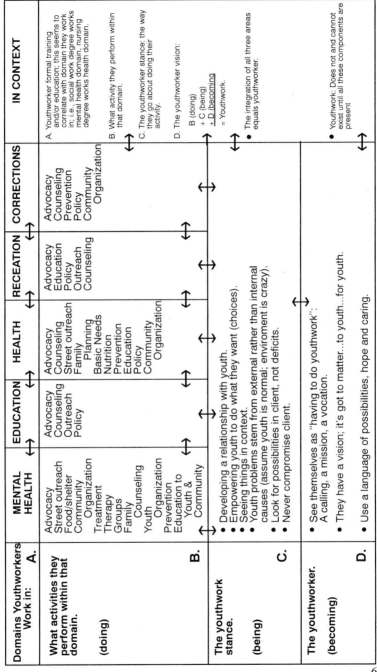

OVERVIEW

The combination of becoming, doing, and being in detached youth-work is portrayed in Figure 1 (page 67). This, the interviews teach us, is the essence of youthwork to those who become youthworkers, who do youthwork, and who are in their very essence detached youthworkers.

NOTE

6. This study was done in Minnesota, where Lutheran religious values and lan-guage are insinuated into everyday, secular speech. Luther's stance on vocation is very important theologically, and his conceptions are widely held among youth and adults (Baizerman, 1998).

Chapter V

Discussion–
What Does It Mean?

A major purpose of this study was to learn about detached youth-work–what it is, who does it, how, where, and with whom it is done, how its practitioners come to this work, and their training and supervision on the job. A second purpose was to learn what detached youthwork means to its practitioners–how they perceive and understand their practice, how they live their vocation. A third purpose was the search for the phenomenological essentials of detached youthwork; the core structure of this praxis. All that was learned and found in these areas fits well with earlier studies of detached youthwork, while adding to and deepening that literature, as is detailed in the discussion that follows.

HISTORICAL DETACHED YOUTHWORK

Current detached youthwork in the Twin Cities is both similar to and different from historical detached youthwork. It will be recalled that early U.S. detached youthwork–in New York City, Chicago, Boston, and Los Angeles in the 1950s and 1960s–was characterized by adult male workers employed by public or private social service agencies to work with adolescent male gangs. Early workers practiced a form of social group work (e.g., Konopka, 1972) and had as a primary goal turning the group to pro-social activities while at the same time

[Haworth co-indexing entry note]: "Discussion-What Does It Mean?" Thompson, Jacquelyn Kay. Co-published simultaneously in *Child & Youth Services* (The Haworth Press, Inc.) Vol. 19, No. 2, 1999, pp. 69-82; and: *Caring on the Streets: A Study of Detached Youthworkers* (Jacquelyn Kay Thompson) The Haworth Press, Inc., 1999, pp. 69-82. Single or multiple copies of this article are available for a fee from The Haworth Document Delivery Service [1-800-342-9678, 9:00 a.m. - 5:00 p.m. (EST). E-mail address: getinfo@haworthpressinc.com].

providing pro-social opportunities for individual members. The longer the worker remained in the neighborhood, the more involved he became in community organization activities and in dealing with other local problems.

Early detached youthworkers were not explicitly trained for this work, but most had social service experience, typically with youth. Most had grown up in neighborhoods similar to the ones in which they worked. Supervision was by a master's degree level social worker-on paper and occasionally in reality. Workers tended to drift into and out of this work, the latter following what is now called "burnout." Recruitment was easy, retention difficult.

Early detached youthwork was done "on the street," "where the kids were." It was a reaching out, leaving the agency building to enter the environment-the world-of the gang. It was ideally an ecologically sensitive intervention, one designed with knowledge about adolescents (males), delinquency, gangs, "the street," and working and lower class culture. It was also, at times, driven at least in theory by academic theories of juvenile delinquency etiology and derivative control and preventive intervention strategies, the key intervention being the relationship between the worker and the youth.

Much of this picture of early detached youthwork could pass for a modern photo, with three major exceptions: Current youthworkers do not work with gangs of youth; rather, they work with individual "alienated" youth on the street or with groups of youth who have been identified as having similar problems (e.g., AIDS or being involved in prostitution). Like traditional youthworkers, they become more involved in a variety of problems, both on the individual and the community level, the longer they remain in the area. Second, agencies today tend not to have an explicit belief in the intrinsic value of detached youthwork, but rather see it as a "recruiting tool" for agency programs (with one local exception). Third, women are now commonly found among detached youthworkers, as well as among clients.

THE ESSENCE OF DETACHED YOUTHWORK

The basic question that drove this study was, "What is detached youthwork?" That is, "Who does what to whom, when, how, and why, using what auspices, which skills, and what authority?" The simple answer is: It depends!

Detached youthwork, in essence, was found to be a *stance* that is actualized as a particular praxis depending on the unique moment-the unique youth in a unique context. Detached youthwork thus is contingent: It depends. Hence there is no single method, skill, or approach, but there are commonalities that constitute its essence. These are presented as:

* *Becoming* (The Vision of Detached Youthwork);
* *Doing* (The Context of Detached Youthwork); and
* *Being* (The Stance of Detached Youthwork).

Becoming: The Vision

Youthworkers had a difficult time telling how they came to be in youthwork. It reminded me of when I interviewed young women sixteen years ago and asked how they got into prostitution. Like the youthworkers, they had a hard time talking about it, other than by giving me events that led up to their involvement. They never said that they decided (i.e., consciously) to become involved. The youthworkers never decided to become youthworkers, either, much less detached youthworkers. They talked about some private sense they had about wanting to work with kids and, thus, to work in the helping professions. Their most common first response was, "I don't know," then, "God, this is hard! I never thought about it."

When I asked, "How long have you been doing youthwork?" most responded by asking me what "counts" as youthwork or asking me to explain what I meant. Did working with mentally retarded kids or in a treatment center or a recreational facility count as youthwork? When I responded, "When do you think you became a youthworker?" long pauses usually followed. They would then answer by listing jobs where the title was youthworker, child care worker or the like.

Thus, their responses were not really answers. At best, they could reconstruct a history. For most, becoming a youthworker had not been a conscious choice or even a decision but instead the result of a series of events or jobs that led them to their present job in detached youthwork. These events and jobs were themselves not necessarily actively sought or chosen. It was the things they liked about youthwork-such as the style or freedom-or the things they disliked about other jobs-such as the work, structure, and philosophy-that were the primary influences in their entering youthwork.

Probing brought forth a deeper, more authentic answer: "Someone was there for me when I was a kid," or "There was no one there for me when I was young." These answers fit with the workers as people and with the detached youthworker style. Deep personal insight is not part of the ethos, nor is "the past." Indeed, the very question points in the wrong direction: Detached youthwork is practiced "in the here and now." Like the streets, it is concrete, specific, practical and immediate.

The youthworkers' seeming lack of insight could also be a result of their lack of training, including the absence of a language to articulate how they came to be a detached youthworker. Since it is not a profession and is barely an occupation, there are no established formal or informal paths to becoming a youthworker and to doing detached youthwork. In the United States, youthwork and its detached form are job titles more than occupations. Hence it is difficult to define when one is a youthworker or is doing youthwork and, without a formal training program, to know when one is no longer "becoming" a youthworker.

Accepted professions such as psychology have career stages. One knows when one is a psychologist. One knows what knowledge, skills, and attitudes constitute the profession. It is a priori; an institutionalized process. Statements such as, "I am going to school to become a psychologist" and "I am interning as a psychologist" make sense. It does not make sense to say "I am going to school to be a youthworker" because there are no such schools and because there is no consensus about what youthwork is and, hence, what one needs to know, believe, and do as a youthworker. Thus, as they perceive it, one can never arrive and be certified. One simply works with youth. The absence of an institutionalized profession with its cultures of education, practice, language, myths, history and symbols makes the seemingly simple question of why one is a youthworker ambiguous and difficult to answer.

Among other possible explanations for the workers' apparent lack of insight is that for them the issue is not important; it is so mundane, so natural, that it is difficult to distance oneself and to explain it to someone else.[7] Then there is the possibility that, being more comfortable with hands-on "doing," they tend to be relatively inarticulate. What is seen, then, is that while the social process of becoming a detached youthworker is somewhat clear, job to job to job, event to job, etc., the motivations for doing so are far less clear. Unclear, too, are the reasons and the accounts offered by the workers.

Interviewing these adults was most often like interviewing an early (ages 12-14) or middle (15-17) adolescent. Most were concrete, ahistorical, and focused on the "now." This the youth, the worker, and the streets have in common. Neither abstractly thinking intellectuals nor highly trained, moderately concretely thinking professionals could (or do) survive working on the streets. Since most workers had been "on the streets" for at least two years, I may have interviewed fully socialized street people who like the youth, do not spend a lot of time on "yesterday": "The beat goes on," in the song, in the streets, and in their lives.

Doing: The Context

Detached youthworkers are also not articulate about what they do. It is more than the content that is at issue here, more than the historical, more than limited personal insight, more than the inaccessible mundane. It may be their "natural inability," it may, again, reflect street culture, or it may reflect the absence of a developed culture of detached youthwork. In any event, their responses were short and seemingly incomplete.

"What is it you do?" I asked. "I do intake," "I do street outreach," "I do therapy," they answered. They do activities, actions, events, and categories of activities. Their world is organized in the activities of the worlds in which they work. Youthwork is the doing of the activities. Which activities? Whose activities?

Detached youthwork is doing "what needs to be done" for youth in the contexts of the adult-run "helping" agencies. Their first answer is bureaucratic, from the employee perspective. Then, with probing, they respond from the youth advocate perspective. Perspectives change as the worker's stance changes–the worker's answer to the question, "What do you do?" is, again, a simple but profound and telling one: It Depends.

Detached youthwork as a praxis is "youth-in-context" driven, and always contingent. Basic is "relationship," worker to youth. Ideally, it is worker, youth, and social agencies, police, courts, and the like. Doing "it-depends" work depends on developing relationships. This is both practice philosophy and existential fact. Without relationships, nothing gets done and nothing can be expected to get done. Hence, detached youthwork is, on one level, the creation, sustenance, and "manipulation" of relationships. The currency of detached youthwork is relationships.

The Detached Youthwork Relationship: The Essence of Doing

By relationship, the workers mean "being there" in an authentic way for the youth. It is forming relationships not because it is the professionally "right" thing to do, but rather because it is the *human* "right" thing to do and a good way to be (Gordon, 1994).

To youth, relationship means "some adult who listens and doesn't abuse or use me," "who helps me get what I need," "who's there when and how I need them" (personal communications with adolescents), while in the context of more formal "youth services" relationship means "fixing" the kid, i.e., making him or her less troublesome to adults and/or engaging him or her in pro-social behavior.

Creating Relationships. One "creates," "develops," or "builds" relationships. This is done through "hanging out" near and with youth, being geographically as well as psychologically close to the youth and their needs and issues. A relationship is created by waiting, listening, hearing what the youth is saying, and "accepting" the youth as he or she is. It is often developed initially because the youth is physically and/or psychologically in need and the worker "meets that need" without making the youth "jump through hoops" or "pay a price." This is the ideology of detached youthwork in its metaphorical purity.

Sustaining Relationships. Relationships are sustained by "following through," doing what one said one would do, and holding similar expectations of the youth. They are sustained by spending time with the youth, listening, and hearing what he or she is saying. A relationship is sustained by focusing on possibilities, creating opportunities to move toward the possible, and accepting movement "forward and backward."

"Manipulating" Relationships. The relationship between the youth and the detached youthworker is the means by which the youth can attempt new things, experience new feelings (or rediscover old ones), and learn other ways of looking at and living in the world. It is manipulated ideally to achieve "personal growth" and positive changes in the youth's way of doing everyday life.

Relationship as Skill. To the detached youthworker, creating, sustaining, and "manipulating" relationships with youth and adults are their primary skills-although they don't use this word, which is in the language game of professions and their training, classrooms, and "theory," i.e., seen as irrelevant abstractions (Dreyfus & Dreyfus, 1992). Yet when talking about their work (themselves working; themselves at work), youthwork means skill. Relationship is something they know how to do and something they do well. In their metaphor, they "build" relationships.

This, then, is their skill; how, where, when, and with whom it is used show how, where, when, and with whom detached youthwork is practiced (i.e., actualized). Given who these workers choose as youth-clients-street kids-their willingness and ability to create "real relationships" is impressive. It is the major rationale for this kind of youthwork as well as, at times, a clear challenge to other human service professionals. These workers "connect" with the unconnected and (thought to be) unconnectable.

Relationship as "Caring-in-Action." Detached youthwork often finds the metaphorical, theological language of *hope, caring,* and *presence* easier to use than formal, "professional" human service concepts. Thus, relationships are a form of caring; they are "caring-in-action." To these workers, caring is a special idea; for most, the caring of an adult (or its absence) brought them to this work (Eriksson, 1996). Unlike the youth's family or other adults, in their view, they "truly care" for their youth-clients. Because the youthworkers "*truly* care," they believe, these "unreachable youth" respond by "trusting." By trusting the relationship, or so it is hoped, the young people may come to trust the opportunities that are created through this relationship. This is youthwork and human service "theory," really, and also its philosophy and ideology. This sense of caring also feeds the youthworkers' concern for advocacy.

Relationships as Mystical. Sinetar (1986) describes the mystical quality of relationships in her book, *Ordinary People as Monks and Mystics: Lifestyles for Self-Discovery,* as follows:

> A gift of self might be one's application of energy and effort to a vocation in a way which then allows natural talents and aptitudes to be shared with others. . . . the giver experiences a kinship, or a sense of relatedness, to others. This quality is significant because it is impossible to genuinely care for others, without a real sense of involvement with others. (pp. 59-60)

Detached Youthwork: The Mystical Essence as Ideology

Detached youthworkers present themselves and their work as being essentially mystical in the sense just described. This may be a piece of their inarticulateness, but it is likely more. It is detached youthwork presented as having a mystical essence, which is itself a philosophy. Thus, the core of detached youthwork is a philosophy of the mystical nature of relationships.

Unbeknown to most of them, detached youthworkers understand relationships in a similar way to the understanding of those who do existential therapy. Kaplan et al. (1985) summarize this as follows:

No object, person, or event exists without a context. Different aspects of reality are experienced under different circumstances and in different contexts. The person is aware of absolute-real things in others and in the world in a special way: Contextually, intentionally, and meaningfully.

The goals of existential therapy are for the person to utter, clarify, and identify projects; the personal myth to assume owner-ship and responsibility for ones' projects; to validate and to em-brace both the inevitable positive and negative aspects of rela-tionships and of acts so that the divided, unattended parts of the personality become integrated. The attainment of such goals leads to greater autonomy, responsibility and an attendant equali-ty in relationships. Progress toward these goals is sought by means of acceptance, affirmation, and authentic relating between therapist and client. Acceptance is not synonymous with uncon-ditional positive regard.

Authentic acceptance can occur only when the therapist sees the person as having chosen for the best of all possible reasons. Further, clarity demands that acts are seen as intentional, that each choice carries its own negative consequences and that those tend to be denied by self-blame.

It is contradictory to accept persons as they are and simulta-neously to work for their change. By working for movement, change, actualization, mental health, or adjustment however de-fined, one is in danger of reinforcing the person's self-deception.

Persons are in precisely the state they should be in. If they believed that they would be better off in some other position, they would be there. Many persons, however, want to deny the negative aspects of the state they have chosen. (pp. 1441-43)

"It Depends" Means (in Part) that I Can't Tell You What I Do

If what the detached youthworker does "depends," how can youthworkers be expected to tell you what they do? Each youth, each moment is unique, a story in itself. Yes, there are commonalities and patterns, but they are abstractions. The concrete, specific is what matters. Here too, and unknowingly, the detached youthworker speaks like an Existentialist: It depends on the meaning, the moment, the choice, and the action: "Let me tell you a story."

And You Can't Supervise Me. "Out of sight, out of mind," as the saying goes. This is true for detached youthworkers, while the agency personnel expected to supervise them act on the adage, "Visibility is accountability." The more time the youthworkers spent with youth and the less time with agency staff, the more likely they were to "identify" with the youth. The long hours of listening, observing, and being with youth create the belief in the youthworker that he or she is one of the few adults who can "really" understand the youth. They begin to look at the agency as if they themselves are outsiders, questioning policies, procedures, and even the beliefs of other agency staff. A vicious cycle frequently arises as the supervisor worries and "frets" about what he or she imagines is happening and why and the resulting anger and frustration of the workers increases those concerns.

The youthworkers saw supervision as woefully inadequate, either absent or as designed to control, confine, or otherwise add more bureaucratic red tape to their lives. Yet they talked of the need for good supervision and for time to reflect with others, perhaps with the supervisor as a guide.

To them, supervision is best when it is "mentoring"-a teaching, sustenance kind of helping. To the agencies, supervision often meant "control," which often leads to worker defiance. It is in supervision that the worker and supervisor most closely mirror the situation of the youth and his or her troubles with the adult world.

The sources of this tension are structural (worker vs. "boss"), stylistic ("hang-loose" ethic of the worker vs. administrative constraints), and personal (e.g., some workers have difficulty with being controlled and some supervisors need to feel that the are in control). It is also cultural, in that few supervisors were themselves detached youthworkers and, hence, have legitimacy in the eyes of the detached youthworker or practical knowledge to teach the worker, nor do the supervisors see the workers as professional colleagues.

Detached youthworkers may have psychological insight about themselves and/or their clients. Even if such insights are present, however, the workers may still lack a theoretical base for understanding them and their wider significance and a language with which to talk about them. Therefore, supervision–which is often about what it may be within the worker that is influencing what he or she is doing–can be threatening. Further, the supervisor represents the employing agency, and the detached youthworker tends to be in tension with his or her employer. Thus, the very ethos of detached youthwork, the lack of formal preparation, and the personal limitations of the worker all contribute to making their relationship with supervisors difficult.

Detached youthwork is not a profession, then; it is an occupation, a job title, a vocational calling. Using the youthworkers' words, it is a process, a *doing*. The process is focused on self-other relationships, and this constitutes the largest part of its doing.

Detached youthworkers are in essence those who spend their nights and days with youth, "doing relationships" in the service of youth depending on the youth and his or her issues, situation, needs and wants. It is the most basic of human activities: caring for others, although a class of particular others. There is everything and nothing special about this; it is simply a socially organized way to do this with youth who are on the streets. But to *be* a detached youthworker is something more.

Being: The Stance

To the youthworker, the work is a calling, a vocation.[8] These are my words, but they capture the powerful commitment to the ethos of detached youthwork as this is grounded in the nature of the kids they work with: the marginal, the unaffiliated, the disaffected, the mythical adolescent-in-rebellion, in pain, and in trouble. Youthworkers feel that they are "special" and that they work with youth in a special way, in unusual places, i.e., doing Romantic caring for the "outsider."

In less poetic imagery, these are fringe people at work in fringe jobs with a fringe population at a fringe salary. In their own adolescence, they were fringe kids in their families. It is of a single cloth: The marginal person in a marginal job working with those who are invisible, troublesome, and seemingly defiant.

Detached Youthwork as a Way of Life

Detached youthwork is portrayed as a way of life, and indeed it is. One works irregular, never ending hours, nights and days. For many, working with these youth colors how they look at all youth, at times being upset that others have more, have it easier, and do not appreciate what they do have. Many find little time that they can call their own and, thus, their personal relationships may suffer contributing to burnout. They are proud that others cannot tell when they are or are not working.

For many of the workers, The Stance–their way of looking at the world and being with others–is consistently how they live. Yet many do not realize the cost of this in terms of their personal growth, development, and everyday lives. They may be blinded (by choice, perhaps) at times, by Romantic notions of service, or even by pathology. At best, detached youthwork may interfere with healthy adult relationships; at worst, it may be a way of avoiding such relationships.

If the essence of youthwork is relationship, then the youthworker is one whose personal essence is defined as being with others. The workers (like all of us, but more often and more intensely) are defined by and through their relationships. It is a self oriented to the "between" (Buber, in Mundackal, 1977, p. 114). For the detached youthworker, more than for most, the self is contingent, personal identity is processual, and all is emerging and emergent.

The Philosophy of Detached Youthwork Practice

Detached youthwork is not low level or paraprofessional psychology, social work, or education. It has some things in common with each of these, but it is different. The differences lie in the dynamic between and among the setting, the population, and the worker.

The detached youthworkers in this study did not articulate a developed philosophy of youthwork or its practice. From their words and adding my own experience, however, a conception of detached youthwork can be derived.

Witness

The presence of a witness "confirms" the client. Confirming the client is different from just showing positive regard and acceptance. Confirmation is to confirm the whole *being*. It is to enter into what Buber (in Mundackal, 1977, p. 129) described as a dialogical relationship and being in the present, the "existential moment," fully with the person. All moments are full of possibilities, there to be lived. A dialogical relationship is the way to find and create possibilities. Possibilities are a germ of hope.

The presence of a youthworker serves as a witness to these young peoples' lives. As a witness to the "system," to other professions, and to society's failures, they become a "social conscience." As they work in and against these systems, the youthworkers can themselves become an issue to the agencies and the community. Since detached youthworkers play an infinite game in a finite world, they rarely fit with any formal system. Detached youthwork is an *aesthetic*.

Carse (1986) described the difference this way:

> There are at least two kinds of games, one could be called finite, the other infinite. A finite game is played for the purpose of winning, an infinite game for the purpose of continuing to play. (p. 3)
>
> The rules of a finite game may not change. The rules of an infinite game must change. (p. 9)
>
> Finite players are serious; infinite players are playful. (p. 14)
>
> Finite players win titles; infinite players have nothing but their names. (p. 26)
>
> Finite players are theatrical; infinite players are dramatic. (p. 16)

Youthworkers work on the margins of "the system," and there they also play by a different set of rules. They work outside their agencies-away from other staff, away from the accountability demanded of others, and away from supervision. They are literally and figuratively "out of sight." Thus they may be invisible and isolated and feel and act like the "Lone Ranger." As has been noted, the tension that exists between the youthworker and his or her agency is similar to the tension that exists between the youth client and his or her family and/or other adults.

At their best, detached youthworkers practice something akin to an existentialist intervention in a youth agency world that is predominantly behavioristic in orientation. This is a source of their effectiveness, and at the same time another source of estrangement from their social agencies and potential colleagues and collaborators therein. What is the practice of detached youthwork found in this study? It is the practice of a way of life.

A crucial question is whether the apparent (and alleged) relative effectiveness of this type of worker doing this type of work with this type of youth in this type of situation would be enhanced or diminished if he or she were to be formally educated and trained in an established human service profession. Should we simply leave things as they are, in the chaotic order of existential emergence? Or must these workers, like others who work with youth, be held accountable in far more rigorous ways for what they do, how, and why? If so, are these reasonable goals, given worker salary, length of tenure and the like?

CONCLUSION

Detached youthwork is paradoxical. It is emergent–both a presence, "being there," and ephemeral; it seems to be invisible in the daylight only to come out at night. This too, is a metaphor for detached youthwork.

Detached youthwork is a subclass of youthwork characterized by a poorly defined (common) practice, no career path, and an unclear mission. It is fashioned by the particular worker in the particular agency context with particular kids in particular situations. In this, it was an odd group to study. In a sense, were I not a detached youthworker myself, I am not sure that I would believe that detached youthwork even exists!

But it does! And the study reported herein sought and described its essence as that is understood by its local practitioners. It is best conceptualized and discussed in the context of *Becoming, Doing*, and *Being*.

NOTES

7. It is, as St. Augustine said of time, that it was clear until he had to explain it to someone.

8. See Appendix E for the participants' responses that were classified as representing "The Youthwork Stance."

Chapter VI

Conclusions and Implications– Where Do We Go from Here?

A genuine dialogue is enacted whenever there is the experience that "there is much to be said to one another." (Sardello, 1975, p. 276)

The experience of interviewing the seventeen detached youthworkers and the initial discussions with the two focus groups revealed that there was, indeed, much to be said to one another. Over 200 hours of dialogue has been recorded and transcribed. From these data has emerged the essentials of detached youthwork. The purpose of the study was to learn about detached youthwork as seen and understood by its practitioners. This having been accomplished, it is time to assess this field of practice and the study and to suggest implications for youthwork and for research about the practice and its practitioners.

RECRUITMENT AND SELECTION

There are no standardized tests or other procedures for selecting detached youthworkers. As a psychologist, I can bemoan this and can choose whether and how to contribute to the development of a more reliable and valid selection process. But I am also a detached youthworker with seventeen years of experience who understands and accepts this work while remaining, in part, in the Romantic detached youthwork tradition.

[Haworth co-indexing entry note]: "Conclusions and Implications–Where Do We Go from Here?" Thompson, Jacquelyn Kay. Co-published simultaneously in *Child & Youth Services* (The Haworth Press, Inc.) Vol. 19, No. 2, 1999, pp. 83-88; and: *Caring on the Streets: A Study of Detached Youthworkers* (Jacquelyn Kay Thompson) The Haworth Press, Inc., 1999, pp. 83-88. Single or multiple copies of this article are available for a fee from The Haworth Document Delivery Service [1-800-342-9678, 9:00 a.m. - 5:00 p.m. (EST). E-mail address: getinfo@haworthpressinc.com].

83

I believe that I can tell when I meet someone who is or would be a good youthworker. I can also tell when I meet someone who would not be a good youthworker, but it is difficult to describe in objective language what the key criteria are. They involve more than traits or behaviors; they include a "presence," a particular energy, a look in the eye, and what is *not* being said. I am aware of a crucial consciousness or connection that is evoked in me when I am with someone who "has it." Maybe the *meeting* allows for that to emerge (Buber, in Mundackal, 1977, p. 116).

I also believe that it is possible to develop a way to tap the crucial elements more systematically. Such an approach would include a series of structured interviews and observations. The observations could include watching someone work with street youth and how the youth respond, and listening to what the candidate sees and does not see and how he or she processes the encounter and reflects on it. A structured interview could be developed using teaching stories, problem solving stories, and questions that would tap into the individual's values, beliefs, and vision. This study tried to identify the crucial elements, and further research on this is needed. Techniques such as structured critical incidents, activity logs, Behavioral Anchored Rating Scales (BARS), and/or psychological tests such as the Myers-Briggs Type Indicator may be useful.

Discovering and developing youthwork talent may be as creative and difficult a task as is discovering and developing an artist's or a writer's talent. Very often great artists and writers are created in part by great mentors and editors. I would challenge us to find latent, potential youthworkers, to recognize their abilities, to observe and interview them creatively as well as objectively, and to preserve their knowledge and wisdom. Without this, their talents will go unused and lost and detached youthwork will not fully develop its history, its culture, or its practice.

PROFESSIONALIZATION

From a political point of view, "youthwork needs a youthworker or it needs to become its own youthworker." By this I mean it needs to listen to itself, hear what its members are saying, define itself, come to terms with its power, and then go about becoming all it can become. If it is to become a profession, as with all professions, those who would be its members will need to take the lead in defining what it is and what its practice entails.

If I were youthwork's "therapist," my first suggestion would be that it not evaluate itself using the same methods used by other professions. Instead, I would like to see it become the first human service profession that evaluates itself by *human* standards: Compassion, hope, and caring. I urge that it define itself in terms of its core values, not its techniques–that it talk of caring, rather than diagnosis; of hope rather than prognosis; of compassion, rather than techniques and "cures"; of the quality of life, rather than the quantity of clients; of extending its social responsibilities rather than erecting its professional boundaries–and that its success be measured in terms of relationships to clients rather than to sources of funding and institutional support. This would keep its vision, mission, and existential stance in the forefront, where they belong.

I would also suggest that youthworkers find people to listen to them, to document their knowledge, and to help them develop ways to talk about what they do, what they believe, and the ways in which they work. If this were done, it would allow for reflection and the development of a language of youthwork. It would also begin to document the "doing" of youthwork, youthwork practice.

EDUCATION AND TRAINING

Youthworkers perceive themselves as having a *mission* or a *calling*: "Born, not made." It is who they are rather than what they do that matters. This may explain in part their lack of enthusiasm toward formal education. Those I talked to would probably have agreed with Carl Rogers (1957) when he said,

> Intellectual training and the acquiring of information has, I believe, many valuable results, but becoming a therapist is not one of those results. (p. 95)

This Romantic notion may have validity for youthworkers as well.

Despite their dislike of formal education, these youthworkers did go to college and most obtained degrees, but they found little there that fit with their current work. They are more like vocational students, artists, musicians, and the like who want practical training, which they rarely get in their agencies but sometimes do get at workshops. As has been noted, they do not actively seek to learn from their supervisors.

Detached youthwork training needed its own unique curriculum; it should not be pre-social work, pre-counseling, or pre-psychology. Basic elements should include a multi-disciplinary approach to youthwork, specially designed experiential activities, and focused, vigorous exploration of one's own values, beliefs, and attitudes. An effective approach appropriate to their learning styles would involve mentors, as is found in the handcrafts. One of the purposes of the training experience would be to move toward what Maslow (1971) described as the actualized person's attitude toward work:

> . . . in all cases, at least in our culture, they are dedicated people, devoted to some task "outside themselves," some vocation or duty or beloved job. Generally, the devotion and dedication is so marked that one can fairly use the old words vocation, calling, or mission. (p. 301)

SUPERVISION

In the realm of supervision, there are a number of concerns, the most important being the lack of a common understanding of supervision between the worker and the agency. From the perspective of the detached youthworkers, there is a lack of helpful supervision and too much emphasis on accountability and control; the perception on the part of the agencies is that the supervision of youthworkers is difficult (i.e., what they do is poorly defined, they are hard to control, accountability is difficult, etc.).

Youthworkers appear to be open to and even wanting to be supervised if the process is reflective, supportive, and provides a means to remove barriers and obstacles to effective services to client youth. They want someone to talk to about what they are experiencing, someone who will listen, challenge, confront, and accept. They need, in my opinion, supervision that facilitates the development of practical mastery, helps them put their experiences into personal and work contexts, and moves comfortably and regularly between the theoretical level and that of the "real and concrete."

It is important that agency personnel recognize and acknowledge the value of detached youthwork as understood from the perspective of the worker. Administrators must come to understand the inherent structural sources of job strain: The anti-technocratic ideology; the lack of an identified code of ethics; the lack of professional identification and status; the relative isolation; the long hours; and the constant struggle to do the right thing in the right way while being a good person. With such an understanding, administrators could help to prevent burnout and help workers to define appropriate role boundaries. They could also provide outside consultants for detached youthworkers, encourage ongoing meetings among youthworkers employed at different agencies, and provide a variety of other opportunities for effective peer supervision.

RESEARCH IMPLICATIONS

Further research into the *doing* of detached youthwork could facilitate the development of selection criteria and training curricula. Such research would be most useful if it were done using an anthropological participant-observer approach in the actual work situation rather than primarily through interviews or standardized tests. Youthworkers see so much of what they do as "ordinary" and hence not important to mention that perhaps only a relative outsider can perceive what of it is truly ordinary and what is, in fact, extraordinary.

It would also be helpful to have research on the youth with whom detached youthworkers work, not only about who they are, where they come from, and their "problems," but also about how they perceive agencies, detached youthworkers, the "street," and themselves. Without these understandings, the picture remains incomplete.

Additional research on detached youthworkers could be done using classical personality testing, which may prove valuable in conjunction with phenomenological understandings. A more interesting and perhaps more productive approach would include tests for creativity.

Finally, given the wide and apparently expanding "street kids" phenomenon in other cities in the United States and worldwide, additional research is needed to learn about detached youthwork and what youthworkers can learn from their counterparts elsewhere.

INTERNATIONAL IMPLICATIONS

Both in the "developing" countries and in the "developed" world, there are many thousands of children and youth on and of the streets.

In both, detached youthworkers have a central role to play as ambassadors from the adult world, a role that has been actualized to varying degrees in different countries in both the developed and the developing worlds. The present study reflects the state of the field here in the United States, and there are interesting and significant similarities and contrasts, for example, with the situation in Brazil (Chalhub-Oliveira, 1995; deOliveira, 1994). The next step should be to enhance the linkages among youthworkers, academics, and other human service professions across cultures so that relevant information can be shared, discussed, understood, and used. Cross-cultural research is needed to illuminate commonalities and differences among youthworkers and the youth they serve and the implications for effective practice.

CONCLUSION:
THE PRICE YOU PAY
TO WEAR TENNIS SHOES TO WORK

It is hoped that on the basis of the understandings gleaned from this study, the "price" one pays to wear tennis shoes to work can be reduced or shared with others in the human services and in the community.

References

Ackely, E. G., & Fliegal, B. (1960). A social work approach to street-corner girls. *Social Work*, *5*(4), 27-36.

Aichhorn, A. (1935). *Wayward youth.* New York: Viking Press.

Anglin, J. P., Denholm, C. J., Ferguson, R. V., & Pence, A. R. (Eds.). (1990). *Perspectives in professional child and youth care.* New York: The Haworth Press, Inc. (Also published as a special issue of *Child & Youth Services*, 1990, *13*(1/2).)

Austin, D. M. (1957). Goals for gang workers. *Social Work*, *2*(4), 43-50.

Baizerman, M. (1988, November). Do we need detached youthworkers to work with street kids? *Street Children Update: Briefing.*

Baizerman, M. (1989). *Homeless: Neither a profession nor an employee offer shelter or a place to go.* Unpublished manuscript.

Baizerman, M. (1998). *The call to responsible selfhood: The vocational in the lives of youth.* Final Report of the Project on Vocation, Work, and Youth Development. Indianapolis: The Lilly Endowment.

Baizerman, M., & Hirak, J. (1980). *Images of delinquency in Twin Cities newspapers.* Miscellaneous Report 169. St. Paul, MN: University of Minnesota Agricultural Experiment Station.

Baizerman, M., & Thompson, J. (1979). Adolescent prostitution. *Children Today* (U. S. Children's Bureau), *8*(5), 20-24.

Baizerman, M., & Thompson, J. (1981, July/August). Adolescent prostitution research and program update. *Children Today* (U.S. Children's Bureau).

Beker, J., & Baizerman, M. (1982, April). Professionalism in child and youth care and the content of the work: Some new perspectives. *Journal of Child Care*, *1*(1), 11-20.

Bensman, F., & Lilienfeld, R. (1973). *Craft and consciousness: Occupational technique and the development of world images.* New York: John Wiley.

Bergantino, L. (1986). *Psychotherapy, insight and style: The existential moment.* Northvale, NJ: Jason Aronson, Inc.

Bernstein, S. (1964). *Youth on the streets: Work with alienated youth groups.* New York: Association Press.

Bersoff, D. N. (1976). Therapists as protectors and policemen: New roles as a result of Tarasof. *Professional Psychology*, *7*(3).

Beyer, M., & Purita, P. (1978). *It's me again: An aftercare manual for youth workers.* Washington, D.C.: National Youth Alternatives Project, Inc.

Binswanger, L. (1963). *Being-in-the-world.* (Jacob Needleman, transl.). New York: Harper and Row.

Bishops, A. H., & Scudder, J. R., Jr. (1990). *The practical, moral, and personal sense of nursing: A phenomenological philosophy of practice.* Albany, NY: State University of New York (SUNY) Press.

Blake, M. (1961). Youth workers and the police. *Children, 6*(5), 170-174.

Bloch, H. A., & Niederhoffer, A. (1958). *The gang.* New York: Philosophical Library.

Bogdan, R. C., & Biklen, S. K. (1982). *Qualitative research for education: An introduction to theory and methods.* Boston: Allyn and Bacon.

Boxill, N. A. (1990). *Homeless children: The watchers and the waiters.* New York: The Haworth Press, Inc. (Also published as *Child & Youth Services, 14*(1), 1990.)

Brandon, D. (1976). *Zen in the art of helping.* New York: Dell Publishing Co., Inc.

Brockelman, P. T. (1980). *Existential phenomenology and the world of ordinary experience: An introduction.* Landover, MD: University Press of America.

Browler, M. (1988). Gang violence: Color it real. *People Weekly, 29*(17), 42-47.

Brunswick, M. (1990, July 22). Now dealing in drugs and violence, gangs are blamed more for bloodshed. *Minneapolis Star Tribune,* pp. 1A, 12A-13A.

Campbell, A. (1984). *The girls in the gang.* New York: Basil Blackwell, Ltd.

Caplan, N. S., Deshaies, D. J., Suttles, G. D., & Mattick, H. W. (1963, August 26). *The nature, variety and patterning of street club work.* Paper presented at meeting of the Committee on Crime and Delinquency of the Society for the Study of Social Problems and the Section on Criminology of the American Sociological Association.

Caplan, N. S., Deshaies, D. J., Suttles, G. D., & Mattick, H. W. (1964). Factors affecting the process and outcome of street club work. *Sociology and Social Research, 48,* 207-219.

Carse, J. P. (1986). *Finite and infinite games: A vision of life as play and possibility.* New York: The Free Press, A Division of Macmillan, Inc.

Cavan, R. S. (Ed.). (1964). *Readings in juvenile delinquency.* Philadelphia: J. B. Lippincott Company.

Chalhub-Oliveira, T. (1995). *Being with street children: Political, romantic, and professional lived experiences in youthwork.* Unpublished doctoral dissertation, University of Minnesota, Minneapolis.

Childhope. (1989). *Mobilizing community action for street children.* Report of the First Regional Conference/Seminar on Street Children in Asia. Manila: Childhope.

Claxton, G., & Ageha, A. (1981). *Wholly human: Western and eastern visions of the self and its perfection.* London: Routledge and Kegan Paul.

Cloward, R. A., & Ohlin, L. E. (1960). *Delinquency and opportunity.* Illinois: The Free Press of Glencoe.

Coffield, F., & Boirrill, C. (1983). Entree and exit. *The Sociological Review, 31*(3), 520-545.

Colaizzi, P. F. (1970). In *Psychology as a human science, Volume 1.* Duquesne studies in phenomonological psychology. Pittsburgh: Duquesne University Press.

Colaizzi, P. F. (1973). *Reflections and research in psychology.* Dubuque, Iowa: Kendall Hunt.

Colaizzi, P. F. (1975). Technology in psychology and science. In A. Giorgi, C. T.

Fischer, & E. L. Murray (Eds.), *Duquesne studies in phenomenological psychology: Volume II*. Pittsburgh: Duquesne University Press.

Colaizzi, P. F. (1978). Psychological research as the phenomenologist views it. In R. Valle & M. King (Eds.), *Existential phenomenological alternatives for psychology*. New York: Oxford.

Coles, R. (1989). *The call of stories: Teaching and the moral imagination*. Boston: Houghton Mifflin Company.

Cottle, T. J. (1971). *The abandoners*. Boston, MA: Little Brown and Co.

Cressey, D. R., & Ward, D. A. (1969). *Delinquency, crime, and social process*. New York: Harper & Row.

Darou, W. G. (1985). Improving the work environment of youth workers. *Canadian Counselor, 19*(3-4), 183-185.

Dass, R., & Gorman, P. (1988). *How can I help?* New York: Alfred A. Knopf.

Davies, B. (1978). Will youth work endure? *Times Educational Supplement, 3277*(15), 32-39.

deOliveira, W. (1994). *We are on the streets because they are on the streets: The emergence of praxis of street youthwork in Sao Paulo, Brazil*. Unpublished doctoral dissertation, University of Minnesota, Minneapolis.

Dimenstein, G. (1991). *Brazil: War on children*. London: Latin American Bureau (Research and Action) Ltd. (New York: Monthly Review Press).

Dreyfus, H. L., & Dreyfus, S. E. (1992). What is moral maturity? Toward a phenomenology of ethical expertise. In J. Ogilvy (Ed.), *Revisioning philosophy*. Albany, NY: State University of New York (SUNY) Press.

Dumpson, J. D. (1949). An approach to antisocial street gangs. *Federal Probation, 13*(7), 22-29.

Eriksson, H. G. S. J. (1996). *Lived experience of caring in a juvenile justice institution: Towards a new emphasis in child and youth care work*. Unpublished doctoral dissertation, University of Minnesota, Minneapolis.

Etzioni, A. (1969). *The semi-professions and their organization: Teachers, nurses, and social workers*. New York: The Free Press.

Fewster, G. (Ed.). (1990). *Being in child care*. New York: The Haworth Press, Inc. (Also published as *Child & Youth Services, 14*(2), 1990.)

Filstead, W. J. (Ed.). (1970). *Qualitative methodology: Firsthand involvement with the social world*. Chicago: Markham Publishing Co.

Franck, F. (1981). *Art as a way: A return to the spiritual roots*. New York: The Crossroad Publishing Company.

Frank, S., Cosey, D., Angevine, J., & Cardone, L. (1985). Decision making and job satisfaction among youth workers in community based agencies. *American Journal of Community Psychology, 13*(3), 269-287.

Frankl, V. (1967). *Psychotherapy and existentialism: Selected papers on logotherapy*. New York: Simon and Schuster.

Freeman, B. A. (1956). *Techniques of a worker with a corner group of boys*. Thesis submitted to the Boston University School of Social Work.

Friedman, M. S. (1959). Martin Buber's theology and religious education. *Religious Education, 54*, p. 5-17.

Friedman, M. S. (1976). Healing through meeting: A dialogical approach to psychotherapy and family therapy. In J. Smith (Ed.), *Psychiatry and the humanities* (pp. 191-233). New Haven, CT: Yale University Press.

Friedman, M. S. (1978). *Encounter on the narrow bridge: Milestones in the life of Martin Buber.* New York: E. P. Dutton.

Friedman, M. S. (1983). *The confirmation of otherness in family, community, and sociology.* New York: The Pilgrim Press.

Friedman, M. S. (1985). *The healing dialogue in psychotherapy.* New York: Jason Aronson.

Gardner, R. M. (1983). *Self inquiry.* Boston, MA: Little Brown and Co.

Garfinkel, H. (1967). Good sociological reasons for bad clinical records. In *Studies in ethnomethodology.* Englewood Cliffs, NJ: Prentice-Hall.

Geertz, C. (1979). From the native's point of view: On the nature of anthropological understanding. In P. Rabinow & W. M. Sullivan (Eds.), *Interpretative social science.* Berkeley: University of California Press, 1979.

Gillham, J., Bersani, C., Gillham, D., & Vesalo, J. (1979). Workers handling errant youth: A field experiment on effects of inservice training. *Evaluation Quarterly, 3*, 347-383.

Giorgi, A. (1960). *Existential psychology.* New York: Random House, Inc.

Giorgi, A. (1970). *The approach to psychology as a human science.* New York: Harper and Row.

Giorgi, A. (1971). A phenomenological approach to the problem of meaning and serial learning. In A. Giorgi, W. Fischer, & R. von Eckartsberg (Eds.), *Duquesne studies in phenomenological psychology I.* Pittsburgh, PA: Duquesne University Press.

Giorgi, A., Fischer, C., & Murray E. (Eds.). (1975). *Duquesne studies in phenomenological psychology II.* Pittsburgh, PA: Duquesne University Press.

Giorgi, A. (Ed.). (1985). *Phenomenology and psychological research.* Pittsburgh, PA: Duquesne University Press.

Glasser, W. (1960). *Mental health or mental illness? Psychiatry for practical action.* New York: Harper and Row.

Glatzer, N. N. (Ed.). (1966). *The way of response: Martin Buber.* New York: Schocken.

Gordon, D. (1994). The ethics of ambiguity and concealment around cancer. In P. Benner (Ed.), *Interpretive phenomenology: Embodiment, caring, and ethics in health and illness* (pp. 279-317). Beverly Hills, CA: Sage Publications.

Gordon, R. A., Short, J. F., Jr., Cartwright, S., & Strodtbeck, F. L. (1963). Values and gang delinquency: A study of street-corner groups. *The American Journal of Sociology, 69*(2), 109-123.

Gould, J., & Kolb, W. (Eds.). (1964). *Dictionary of the social sciences.* New York: United Nations Educational, Scientific, and Cultural Organization (UNESCO).

Grandy, R. (1959). *Evaluation of the Chicago Hyde Park Youth Project.* Chicago: Hyde Park Youth Project.

Guthrie, A. D. (1974). For the street scene: Mobile medical care. *The Journal of Social Issues, 30*(1), 173-180.

Hagedorn, J. M. (1988). *People and folks: Gangs, crime, and the underclass in a rustbelt city.* Chicago: Lakeview Press.

Hamilton, S. E., & Brownell, D. (1973). Dilemmas of an infant profession. *The Australian and New Zealand Journal of Sociology*, 9(3), 54-58.

Hanson, K. (1964). *Rebels in the streets: The story of New York's girl gangs.* Englewood Cliffs, New Jersey: Prentice-Hall, Inc.

Harper, R. (1972). *The existential experience.* Baltimore: The Johns Hopkins University Press.

Heschel, A. J. (1965). *Who is man?* Stanford, CA: Stanford University Press.

Hillman, J. (1975). *Re-visioning psychology.* New York: Harper and Row.

Husserl, E. (1977). *Phenomenological psychology* (John Scanlon, transl.). The Hague: Nijhoft.

Independent Commission on International Humanitarian Issues. (1986). *Street children: A growing urban tragedy.* A report for the Independent Commission. London: Weidenfeld and Nicolson.

Jeffs, T., & Smith, M. (1987). *Youth work.* Houndmills, England: Macmillan Education, Ltd.

Johnson, R. E. (1971). *Existential man: The challenge of psychotherapy.* New York: Pergamon Press.

Johnson, R. E. (1976). *In quest of a new psychology: Toward a redefinition of humanism.* New York: Human Sciences Press.

Juvenile Delinquency Evaluation Project. (1960). *Dealing with the conflict gang in New York City: Interim report no. XIV.* New York: Juvenile Delinquency Evaluation Project of New York City.

Kaplan, H., & Sadock, B. (Eds.). (1985). *Textbook in psychiatry.* Baltimore: Williams and Wilkins.

Kephart, W. M. (1976) *Extraordinary groups: The sociology of unconventional lifestyles.* New York: St. Martin's Press.

Kiesow, J. A. (1973). *Role model for the paraprofessional youthworker in the extension service.* Washington, D.C.: Extension Service.

Klein, M. W. (Ed.). (1967). *Juvenile gangs in context: Theory, research, and action.* Englewood Cliffs, N.J.: Prentice-Hall, Inc.

Kobrin, S. (1959). The Chicago Area Project: A 25 year assessment. *Annals of American Academy of Political and Social Science, 322,* 19-29.

Koch, S. (1959). Some trends of study, I. In S. Koch (Ed.), *Psychology: A study of a science, Vol. 3.* New York: McGraw-Hill.

Konopka, G. (1972). *Social group work: A helping process.* Englewood Cliffs, N.J.: Prentice-Hall, Inc.

Krippenhoff, K. (1980). *Content analysis: An introduction to its methodology.* Beverly Hills: Sage Publications.

Kvaraceus, W. C., & Miller, W. B. (1959). *Delinquent behavior, culture, and the individual.* Washington: National Education Association, pp. 77-79.

Laing, R. D. (1976). *Do you love me?* New York: Pantheon Books.

Lamar, J. V., Jr. (1988). A bloody West Coast story. *Time, 131*(32), 32-35.

Lefkowitz, B. (1987). *Tough change: Growing up on your own in America.* New York: The Free Press.

Lerman, P. (1958, October). Group work with youth in conflict. *Social Work, 3*(4), 71-77.

Lerner, M. (1957). *America as a civilization.* New York: Simon and Schuster.

Livingston, E. (1987). *Making sense of ethnomethodology.* London: Routledge & Kegan Paul.

Los Angeles County, California. (1965). The correctional costs of serviced and unserviced juvenile gangs: An evolution of a detached worker program. Los Angeles: Office of Research, Department of Probation.

MacQuarrie, J. (1973). *Existentialism.* New York: Penguin Books.

Mahrer, A. R. (1978). *Experiencing: A humanistic theory of psychology and psychiatry.* New York: Brunner/Mazel.

Mahrer, A. R. (1987). *Therapeutic experiencing: The process of change.* New York: W. W. Norton and Co.

Maslow, A. H. (1960). *Existential psychology: What's in it for us?* New York: Random House.

Maslow, A. H. (1971). *The farther reaches of human nature.* New York: The Viking Press.

Maxwell, J. (1990). YFL worker claims police harass street youth. *Christianity Today, 34*(4), 42-45.

May, R. (Ed.). (1960). *Existential psychology.* New York: Random House.

May, R. (1967). *Psychology and the human dilemma.* Princeton, New Jersey: D. Van Nostrand Company, Inc.

May, R. (1983). *The discovery of being: Writings in existential psychology.* New York: W. W. Norton and Company.

McWilliams, P. (1970). *I love therefore I am.* Los Angeles: Prelude Press.

Miller, W. B. (1957, December). The impact of a community group work program on delinquent corner groups. *Social Service Review, 31*(4), 396-406.

Miller, W. B. (1958). Lower class culture as a generating milieu of gang delinquency. *Journal of Social Issues, 14*(3), 5-19.

Miller, W. B. (1959). Implications of urban lower class culture for social work. *Social Service Review, 33*(3).

Miller, W. B. (1962). The impact of a "total-community" delinquency control project. *Social Problems,* 10, 168-191.

Miller, W. B. (1965). Violent crimes in city gangs. *Annals of the American Academy of Political and Social Sciences, 64*(March), 97-112.

Misiak, H., & Sexton, V. S. (1973). *Phenomenological, existential and humanistic psychologies: A historical survey.* New York: Grune and Stratton.

Morris, V. C. (1966). *Existentialism in education: What it means.* New York: Harper & Row.

Mundackal, J. (1977). *Man in dialogue: A study of dialogue and interpersonal relationship according to Martin Buber.* Alwaye, Kerla, India: Pontifical Institute Publications.

Myers-Briggs, I., with Myers, P. B. (1980). *Gifts differing.* Palo Alto, CA: Consulting Psychologists Press, Inc.

New York City Youth Board. (1949). Policy manual. New York City Youth Board.

New York City Youth Board. (1952). *Reaching the unreached: Fundamental aspects of the program of the New York City Youth Board.* New York City Youth Board.

New York City Youth Board. (1956). Expansion of the gang project. *Youth Board News, 8*(3). New York City Youth Board.

New York City Youth Board. (1960). *Reaching the fighting gang.* New York City Youth Board.

New York City Youth Board. (1962). *The summer of 1962: A report on New York City's program of vigilance and services for youth.* New York City Youth Board.

New York City Youth Board Research Department. (1965). *The changing role of the street worker in the Council of Social and Athletic Clubs.* New York City Youth Board.

Novak, M. (1970). *The experience of nothingness.* New York: Harper & Row.

Office of Youth Development, U.S. Department of HEW. (1973). *Reaching out with a new breed of worker.* Washington, D.C.: Government Printing Office.

Onions, C. T. (Ed.) *The shorter Oxford English dictionary, 3rd edition.* Oxford: Clarendon Press.

Ornstein, R. E. (1973). *The psychology of consciousness.* San Francisco, CA: W. H. Freeman and Co.

Panko, S. M., & Patterson, B. E. (Eds.). (1976). *Makers of the modern theological mind: Martin Buber.* Waco, Texas: Word Books.

Patton, M. Q. (1980). *Qualitative evaluation methods.* Beverly Hills: Sage Publications.

Philadelphia (PA) Department of Welfare. (1964). *Annual report, 1963.* Youth Conservation Services.

Polkinghorne, D. E. (1988). *Narrative knowing and the human sciences.* Albany, NY: State University of New York (SUNY) Press.

Proceedings: National Youth Workers Conference. (1978). Washington, D.C.: National Youth Alternatives Project, Inc.

Reamer, F. (1982). Conflicts of professional duty in social work. *Social Casework, 63*(10), 579-585.

Redl, F. (1945). The psychology of gang formation and the treatment of delinquents. In *The psychoanalytic study of the child, Vol. I,* pp. 367-377. New York: International Universities Press.

Redl, F., & Wineman, D. (1951). *Children who hate.* Glencoe, Illinois: The Free Press.

Report of the Interregional Seminar on the Training of Professional and Voluntary Youth Leaders, organized jointly by the United Nations, the United Nations Educational, Scientific and Cultural Organization and the Government of Denmark. (1970). New York: The United Nations.

Reynolds, D. K. (1984). *Playing ball on running water: Living Morita psychotherapy–The Japanese way to building a better life.* New York: Quill.

Ritter, B. (1987). *Covenant house: Lifeline to the street.* New York: Doubleday.

Robertson, G., & Erlilck, A. N. (1974). The use of non-professional change agents in an institution. *Canadian Psychiatric Association Journal, 19*(5), 469-472.

Robinson, B. (1990). Mean streets. *Minneapolis-St. Paul Magazine, 18*(5), 65-69.

Rogers, C. R. (1957). The necessary and sufficient conditions of therapeutic personality change. *Journal of Consulting Psychology, 21*(4), 95-103.

Romanyshyn, R. D. (1982). *Psychological life, from science to metaphor.* Austin: University of Texas Press.

Rutter, D. (1984). *Looking and seeing: The role of visual communication in social interaction.* New York: John Wiley & Sons.

Sacks, O. (1984). *A leg to stand on.* New York: Summit Books.

Sardello, R. (1975). Hermeneutical reading: An approach to the classic texts of psychology. In A. Giorgi, C. Fischer, & E. Murray (Eds.), *Phenomenological psychology, Vol. II* (pp. 273-300). Pittsburgh, PA: Duquesne University Press.

Schon, D. (1983). *The reflective practitioner: How professionals think in action.* New York: Basic Books.

Seibert, J. M., & Olson, R. A. (1989). *Children, adolescents and AIDS.* Lincoln, NB: University of Nebraska Press.

Shaw, C., & Jacobs, G. (1940). The Chicago Area Project: An experimental community program for the prevention of delinquency in Chicago. *Proceedings of the American Prison Association, 60*(9), 40-53.

Shertzer, B., & Linden, J. (1979). *Fundamentals of individual appraisal: Assessment techniques for counselors.* Boston, MA: Houghton Mifflin Company.

Shimkin, D. B., & Golde, P. (Eds.). (1983). *Clinical anthropology: A new approach to American health problems?* Lanham, MD: University Press of America.

Siegal, H. (1977). *Street ethnography.* Beverley Hills, CA: Sage Publications.

Silberstein, L. (1989). *Martin Buber's social and religious thought.* New York: New York University Press.

Sinetar, M. (1986). *Ordinary people as monks and mystics: Lifestyles for self-discovery.* Mahwah, NJ: Paulist Press.

Sobesky, W. E. (1976). Youth as child care workers: The impact of stage of life on clinical effectiveness. *Child Care Quarterly, 5*(4), 262-273.

Spergel, I. (1962). A multidimensional model for social work practice: The youth worker example. *Social Science Review, 36,* pp. 62-71.

Spergel, I. (1966). *Street gang work: Theory and practice.* Reading, MA: Addison-Wesley.

Spradley, J. P., & McCurdy, D. W. (1972). *The cultural experience: Ethnography in complex society.* Chicago: Science Research Associates, Inc.

Swart, J. (1990). *Malunde: The street children of Hillbrow.* Johannesburg, Republic of South Africa: Witwatersrand University Press.

Taylor, C. S. (1989). *Dangerous society.* East Lansing, Michigan: Michigan State University Press.

Thrasher, F. M. (1927). *The gang: A study of 1,313 gangs in Chicago.* Chicago: The University of Chicago Press.

Tice, K. (1998). *Tales of wayward girls and immoral women: Case records and the professionalization of social workers.* Urbana: University of Illinois Press.

Tompkins, D. C. (1966). *Juvenile gangs and street groups: A bibliography.* Berkeley, California: Institute of Governmental Studies.

Torrey, E. F. (1986). *Witchdoctors and psychiatrists: The common root of psychotherapy and its future.* Northvale, N.J.: Jason Aronson, Inc.

Van Kaam, A. (1958). *The experience of really feeling understood by a person: A phenomenological study of the necessary and sufficient constituents of this sub-*

jective experience as described by 365 subjects. Unpublished dissertation, Western Reserve University, Cleveland.

Van Kaam, A. (1966). *The art of existential counseling.* Wilkes-Barre, Pa: Dimension Books.

Waltz, H. (1946). Los Angeles Youth Project. *Community Organization for Youth, 1*(4), 12-14.

Watson, G. (1990). Gangs put $5,000 bounty on drug activist's life. *Jet, 77*(38), 38-42.

Watts, A. (1961). *Psychotherapy east and west.* New York: Vintage Books, A Division of Random House.

Watts, A. (1966). *The book on the taboo against knowing who you are.* New York: Collier Books.

Wehr, G. (1988). *Jung, a biography.* Boston, MA: Shambhala.

Weisberg, D. K. (1985). *Children of the night: A study of adolescent prostitution.* Lexington, Massachusetts: D. C. Heath and Company.

Welfare Association of Cleveland. (1959). *A community-wide approach: The United Youth Program, 1954-59.* Cleveland, OH: Cleveland Group Work Council.

Weppner, R. S. (1977). *Street Ethnography.* Beverly Hills: Sage Publications.

Wertz, F. J. (1983). From "everyday" to psychological description: An analysis of moments of a qualitative data analysis. *Journal of Phenomenological Psychology, 14*(2).

Wertz, F. J. (1985). Method and findings in a phenomenological psychological study of a complex life event. In A. Giorgi (Ed.), *Phenomenology of psychological research* (pp. 155-214). Pittsburgh, PA: Duquesne University Press.

Willworth, J. (1990). Fighting the code of silence. *Time, 135*, 59-63.

Winokur, M. (1984). *Einstein: A portrait.* Corte Madera, CA: Pomegrante Artbooks.

Winter, R. (1989). *Learning experience: Principles and practice in action-research.* London: The Falmer Press.

Winterton, J. A., & Rossiter, D. (1973). The community agent and directed change. *Journal of the Community Development Society, 4*(2), 53-63.

Zinsser, W. (1984). *Willie and Dwike: An American profile.* New York: Harper & Row.

Appendix A

Structured Interview Format

I. Descriptive Information
- A. Age
- B. Sex
- C. Formal education
- D. How long have you been doing youthwork?
- E. Who have you worked for?
- F. Career history-how did you end up in youthwork?

II. Description of Current Job
- A. What is your job description?
- B. What do you have to know to do your job?
- C. How did you learn to do your job?
- D. What do you do at work?
- E. Where does your day occur?
- F. Is youthwork a profession? If so, is it different from other professions? If not, what is it?
- G. How do you characterize the kids you work with?

III. Youthwork
- A. What are the rules, guidelines of youthwork?
- B. What is your personal philosophy of youthwork?
- C. How does who you are, your past, and your personality turn up in your work?

IV. Youthworkers
- A. How do you see yourself personally and as a youthworker?
- B. How should a youthworker be selected?
- C. What kind of formal education should a youthworker have?

V. Personal
- A. How did you come to do this work?
- B. How do you get your support?
- C. Have you been in counseling or has there been a significant helping person?
- D. What have you learned about kids/yourself from doing youth work?
- E. How do you spend your discretionary time?

VI. Anything that I missed or should be asking?

Appendix B

Consent Form

I understand that I am participating in a study about Youthworkers. I also understand that at any time during the interview I can stop my participation and request that all information I have provided be returned to me. I am aware of, and give permission for this interview to be taped and I have been assured that my interview will be treated confidentially and will only be published anonymously.

If I have any questions after the interview or if I want to talk about any ideas or feelings which result from this interview, I understand that I can call Jackie Thompson for appropriate follow-up.

Participant   Date   Researcher   Date

Appendix C

Sample Interview

Interview #H[9]

Q: *Just the descriptive stuff of age?*

A: I'm 42.

Q: *And sex is male. Formal education, if any?*

A: Yes, Bachelor of Arts degree at the University of Minnesota.

Q: *In what area?*

A: Major in psychology.

Q: *How long have you been doing youthwork?*

A: For ten years.

Q: *Can you give me kind of a career history, what kinds of jobs?*

A: I first worked for a treatment program, residential treatment program for girls. Then went for about 4 years in a residential shelter program. Then I worked for a year in a community-based program that was doing street outreach, similar to the program I'm in now. That summarizes what I'm doing now, about a year and a half again community-based and doing street outreach.

Q: *Can you give me just a sense of job description, just from your perspective and not what your agency says? Include in that a sense of what you, what a day would look like in the job description.*

A: I see. The way I describe my job is in large part to make myself available to young people. For whatever that might be, whether that be transportation, somebody to talk to, talk with, to advocate, whether that be in court or the facility they may be in, or to advocate in some cases with parents. I see being an advocate for youth as very much a part of what we go into. Describing what I do to advocate for them, I think sometimes a good advocate is not necessarily even-handed. I think to be an advocate for, in this case youth, is to put yourself as best you can in their shoes and in that corner.

Q: *What do you think you'd have to know to do your job? What do you have to know?*

A: I think that there are some things that are hard to describe, that you need to know. The fact that there aren't always clear answers to questions that you face or that we face. You have to know the uncertainty of life in general. More specifically and more technically, I think you do well to have the knowledge or at least the elementary knowledge of how youth are impacted by the legal system and how they are impacted by the various helping professions. You have to be somewhat empathic, to be able to draw upon your youth experiences, your experiences as a young person, to be suited to serve young people.

Q: *Do you think you have to have any kind of sense of youth development or . . .*

A: No. That bothers me. That question bothers me because I studied that at one point and if I were to have to put down on paper everything I know about developmental stages and all of the theories about development, I think I'd be hard pressed to fill up a page, but I think intuitively I may have gleaned resources from that educational experience that I may be drawing on today although it's not foremost in my mind because I think in some ways that could strap me a little bit–having those stages in my mind when I go out to work with young people. I found that young people chronologically, knowing what their chronological age is, doesn't necessarily help and I think some people might be developing on some levels at a much more rapid rate in their life then they are on other levels, so I guess having that information at your fingertips may not be necessary but I think that it's of value to have looked at that information about developmental stages.

Q: *How do you think you learned how to do the work you do?*

A: I think I draw heavily on my experiences as a youth. I think I draw on that a lot. In thinking about this interview today, one of the things that I thought about was that when I was a kid we used to get police to chase us. This was exciting for us. And we could always ditch them. They could never catch us when we got into yards and in between the houses. Until one night there was a new cop on the force and when we ran around behind this house one night he was standing there saying, "Where you going boys?" When I thought about that, I thought about youthwork and how I think sometimes being out in front of youth, so when they come around a corner you're already there, that you understand where they were going and perhaps why they were going where they went, so being out in front of youth I think is important. And that's something that comes directly from my experiences as a young person. There were other individuals, too, who kind of stepped out of the adult world to meet young people and another individual, again a police officer that I knew, had an undying faith in our work and he made it real clear to us–which is different from a lot of other adults. There I gave you two examples of experiences that I had as a young person that I think have given me models for the work that I do today. So I draw very much on my experiences, and I think maybe even more on my experience than on the education.

Q: *Experience both as a kid, and then experience through the years of doing this work?*

A: I think, yes, and even through the years of not doing the work, my life experiences. From the time I was 20 until I was 30, roughly, I was not involved in youthwork, although I was going to school and I think my life experiences have embellished my experiences as a youth and my formal education has also given me resources to put with those youth experiences and my life experiences.

Q: *How would you describe yourself as adolescent or your adolescence?*

A: Misunderstood. I would describe myself as having been misunderstood by others. There were many adults that I encountered when I was a young person who seemed unable to look within me. They got hung up at the surface, what they saw on the surface, and they would come no farther. There was again those individuals who went right on by the surface and seemed to adjust to my humanness. Those people were significant to me and when I think about the work I do today, it is very much those kinds of individuals that I would like to be.

Q: *So, you would see some of the adult persons in your own adolescence as mentors, in a sense, for how you are?*

A: I don't know if they were mentors. I was taking lessons that I don't know if they were teaching.

Q: *What would you say, what was it about those people, was it the information they gave you or was it who they were or what was it about them that made you feel connected in some way to them?*

A: They seemed to have more time for myself and for young people. I saw a clever little sign in a school office the other day and it said

"What part of no don't you understand." That's clever on the surface, it's fun. But, that's the kind of response that many adults would give to a kid with the expectation that the kid doesn't need anything more than no. These adults that I was fond of and were significant in my life, gave explanations or why they were saying no. Often times they were reasonable, logical, well-thought-out reasons that I was able to understand and relate to.

Q: *Them as well as the way they presented the information.*

A: I would think the way that they presented it too. All these people that were significant seemed to have met us on ground that other adults wouldn't go onto. For instance, that police officer that I mentioned who was standing behind, in a darkened backyard of the house. We knew that the police didn't get out of their cars, this guy did. So, in some ways he was presenting himself in a different way and the space that he was willing to go to deliver that information was different. He was willing to come to us. I think, maybe within all those people, again having thought about youthwork, these people seemed to be genuine and they seemed to be sincere. Those are two words that have become important to me over the years, because in the way of feedback that I have gotten relative to youth-work and how I do youthwork, those two words, genuine and sincere, have held a great deal of importance. I think that these people were genuine and sincere, where as, a lot of the other adults that I would encounter didn't seem to have that.

Q: *Okay. Is youthwork a profession?*

A: I think I'd have to have in my mind clearly what definition, how one would define profession. But when I think about profession, I think about a title. That becomes prominent in my mind. Again, I think you would find people within professions who have integrity and people in professions who don't have integrity, so that doesn't seem to capture it.

Q: *How is youthwork different if we operate on the assumption that social work is a profession, psychology is a profession. How is youthwork different from those or similar to them?*

A: I think that the optimal psychiatrist, the optimal psychologist, the optimal youthworker would have to have, would have an extreme fondness for humanity. And as a youthworker I see youth as, as an area of humanity that I have chosen to address. Whereas social workers, psychologists, and psychiatrists might range more through the population than just youth, as a youthworker you would have to be invested in the future, in a future that you may not, will not be a part of, physically. But you have to have a regard for the future, a regard for people who will come and be here after you have gone.

Q: *Why did you choose youthwork, why youthwork when you could be a social worker, psychologist, you could go into a whole lot of other fields and probably get more pay, all that kind of stuff. Why youthwork for you, why do you do it?*

A: Because of the inherent vulnerability of youth. Because of the potential or growth and/or change of youths at that time period.

Q: *You could work with young people probably in schools, as a social worker in school, why work with them in the style of youthwork rather than the style of social work?*

A: When I think about schools, social workers, I think of a kind of narrowing, a focus, a prescription for proceeding a certain way and a lot of other bureaucratic type things that would get in my way. It would deprive me from the flexibility that I feel as a youthworker–some of the latitude that I feel as a youthworker. Some of the freedom I feel as a youthworker.

Q: *What do you think are the rules or guidelines of youthworkers that are probably unspoken, not unspoken but unwritten. Like other professions, like social workers, here is the procedure, here is the formula. Do you think youthwork has any of those kinds of things? Is there something that all youthworkers say, "Here are the rules we all play by; here are the guidelines for youthworkers"? When I'm sitting with a group of people who see themselves as youthworkers and do youthwork, and if somebody were to walk in the room and say, "Here is what I just did with this kid; this is what occurred and here is how I handled it" and there would be a consensus of the people that was the right thing or the consensus of the people that was a dumb thing to do, or wouldn't be how we all would have handled it. Do you know what I'm getting at? What kinds of things are the unspoken, maybe sometimes spoken, but the unwritten and the informal kind of rules and guidelines that all youthworkers say here is what we hold to be true.*

A: I think that I have encountered a diversity of youthworkers. I don't know what might be, I can't think of things. But I can only hope that there would be some things that would be guidelines that should define all youthworkers.

Q: *Sometimes when I have been in conferences, on committees or something, I can tell when somebody opens their mouth and the way they are talking about a subject or the way they present the information about a kid issue, that there's a like thinking going on and I'm thinking, this probably is a youthworker. I mean I can pick one out of a crowd. What are those things, what is it that helps you pick out a youthworker in a crowd or in a room. How do you know them?*

A: I think in youthworkers there would, the tip offs that I would look for, would be an enthusiasm about life, a decided fondness for young people. Those are the things that I would look for.

Q: *A lot of people think youthworkers are rebellious? Do you think that is true?*

A: I don't think that it is necessarily the case. An understanding of the fringes is probably a better way to say it. They would have to be there in order for a person to embrace youth because young people in many cases, particularly those young people in the system that we work in, do occupy those fringes. Both the fringes of their youth culture as well as the fringes in the long run in life.

Q: *What is your personal philosophy?*

A: I think it's made up of a lot of things. Philosophy about the work, I think we mentioned it earlier. I think that there's a value in knowing where young people might step, having an understanding of that place that they would step into. My philosophy again is revealed in when I speak of a fondness for young people, that young people need advocates. My philosophy would have to do, would suggest that I nearly always have the time for a young person. To listen, although I may have heard similar stories many, many times. To always listen as new and fresh as I can. To know that there is a–to believe that there is vast potential in each and every young person that I meet. That the jury is still out on who this person is going to be in life in the long run, no matter what the circumstances have been up to the point that I encounter that youth. In conversations where it's, where the conversation would reflect a collaborative search for answers, for solutions, for understandings. To see youth as every bit as valuable as anybody walking the face of the earth. In the agency we speak in terms of young people as being us, only later and I see the young people very much that way. I see them in me.

Q: *How much do you think who you are, your personality, your past experiences, personal and professional, shows up in how you practice what you do?*

A: I think it shows up everywhere, and my interests, my life experiences, I think, would suggest that I and how I perceive those experiences would perhaps suggest or maybe even predict that there might be a desire in me to reach back to young people coming behind me. Just because of the fact that I think that there is some high ground in life. That has to do with being sensitive to young people–that high ground, it's been my experience, doesn't have a lot of people standing on it. I think for me it's been easy to get there in many ways. It's been easy to find the high ground. It's been easy to go to that high ground, it feels natural. I have a lot of people I don't think are even aware that there is that high ground or a need for anybody to be on that high ground. There may be confusion in the minds of people as to why anybody would entertain the idea of that high ground.

Q: *If you were going to pick, given who you are and how you do this and your philosophies, and I wrote a program, let's say, how would you pick the staff? Personality, education all those kinds of things?*

A: I would want to know what authors they read and which authors they liked. For some reason that has always been important to me, maybe it's just because of its clear absence from any kind of interviewing that I'd seen. When I think about life and how I've come through life, what's been important to me and what I've learned and where I've learned it, literature has been extremely important to me. So, if I could not ask another question of a person, if I could only ask one question, I might ask what books they read and who are their favorite authors.

Q: *What would the ones be that you would consider to be a sign of a good youthworker?*

A: The psychological novels, not having gone to them because they were psychological novels, but because they were a rich story that happened to be psychological in nature. Authors and books that may have, may be a reflection of an intensity of search in life for understanding.

Q: *Which ones would you stay away from? What would be a sign to you that this person, if they said this was my favorite book and this was my favorite author, would be a sign that this is probably not a good youthworker?*

A: Romance kinds of novels.

Q: *What would that tell you, why would that matter?*

A: If in the world of literature, within that world, somebody is finding understandings and themselves within much of what is contemporary or romance-type novels, it would have to suggest to me that the search wasn't very far-ranging or the answers didn't need to be very sophisticated.

Q: *Have you ever been in any kind of counseling yourself? What I'm trying to get at is, if you know what it feels like to be on that end of it. So you have never been a client or anything?*

A: No.

Q: *What have you learned from kids in doing youthwork?*

A: I think perhaps they have certainly taught me patience. I think that in some ways, not from them but by them, through them, I've developed a reverence for life, for humanity.

Q: *A lot of people talk about this kind of work as being a burnout kind of thing. What is it that keeps you in this? The reason that people started doing this is different from the reason they continue it. But what is it that keeps you going?*

A: One of the most important things that have kept me going is the good feedback that I've gotten from kids. I have been validated in the work that I do by kids. That ties in with what first sent me into the sense of gratitude and indebtedness to a few adults that I encountered when I was a young person. I set out to emulate those adults and in some way, possibly, impact young people as an adult as I have been impacted as a young person by those adults. So, when I set out to do that, what I set out to be, somebody who would approach youth, directions that they were not being approached from, I've gotten feedback that has told me that I have succeeded in doing that. I have reinforced, initially, what I went in there to do, to try to do something that I wasn't, didn't have a clear understanding of how it would be done, that's been reinforced for me by the feedback that I've gotten from young people.

So, that I think is what has kept me going. That I have had, and it takes some reading between the lines, too; you don't just come out and say, "Well you've been a very significant person that I need to have happen in my life," and they don't have that. You only have to be able to in some ways glean that from what they're saying and how they might respond to you in certain circumstances. Because, I think, sometimes kids aren't real good at expressing themselves and so you have to try and understand what it is they mean by what they've said.

That's been the most significant thing. That's what's kept me going. I'm refreshed and renewed in the work by this agency and by the way you relate as a supervisor to your staff, because I think I was getting burnt out and frustrated and it was primarily because of administrative things. I haven't run into those administrative obstacles and so I think it's really significant in my career in youth-work, it's been significant coming here. It's given me a second wind that I was becoming desperate for not too long ago. To embellish upon that, I would say that in my mind I had a vision of what, of how people are best supervised. It seems as though what has occurred to me is that the best position for a supervisor to be in is: One, to insulate the line workers from the bureaucracy that is all on the other side of the supervisor. Secondly, clearly carry the needs of the line worker to that bureaucracy.

Q: *That's a nice sense of how it is, being in that position of a youth-worker. That's what I wish, so that's how I pursue it, but I'm not sure what's all there. What I'm trying to figure out, do you think are there any questions that I should be asking that I haven't asked?*

A: I guess, I think you covered much of it. I think that the emphasis on my experiences as a young person was really important. Very much importance in this inquiry.

Q: *I think that's it then, unless you can think of anything else. One of the things that was in here, I think you answered it, but maybe not specifically, is there any reason why the kind of kids you chose to work with versus other kinds of kids? Assuming that there's kinds of problems or whatever but working with kids in a streetwork outreach you work with a certain kind of kid, versus a different kind of kid. Is there something about this kind of kid that's attractive versus another kind?*

A: To begin with, I think in some ways they'll pick me in as much as me picking them. In working residential I saw a lot of young people leave those facilities, run away from those facilities, and coming to this kind of work, street-work, in some ways seem to me to give me an opportunity to go work for those kids that I couldn't before–primarily because of the makeup of the settings. It didn't have to do with me, it didn't have to do with them, it had to do with where we met. So, I felt like being there in a different zone, giving me an opportunity to work with all those kids that I had missed in working in a structured residential setting.

Q: *Okay.*

NOTE

9. Minor editing has been done to the text for purposes of clarification.

Appendix D

Seventeen Analytic Themes

1. Work Activities
2. Working with Kids
3. Supervision
4. Training
5. Ethics
6. Entry into the Field
7. Learning Detached Youthwork
8. What Do You Need to Know to Do Detached Youthwork?
9. What Makes a Good Detached Youthworker?
10. The Youthwork Stance
11. Traits
12. Education
13. Youthwork as a Profession
14. Issues Around Kids
15. Burnout
16. Relationships with the Agency
17. Lifestyle

Yes. Yes. That kind of intuitive, knowing what is what. The other thing that I started to pick up on is that there's a real difference between if somebody is getting better or is not getting better. What is that? It's like, it's so hard to measure that. But it's easy to measure self-destruction. . . . It's like if a kid stops, if a kid moves from cutting themselves more on their arm to upper arm, that's progress. To me if a kid moves from throwing themselves in front of a car to punching a wall, that's progress. And you kind of need to hang in there with them.

They were about healing, help, growth, anything comes to a relationship.

It's sort of a real personal piece for me and maybe this comes up more later in the interview, but I think one of the other things about an effective worker and the piece that I think is important is the whole notion that teenagers are in an impressionable age. And I think they're in an age where you can work with them around some of these Issue like, discrimination and prejudice. They're obviously victims of it all the time. Catch them when they're at this age, try to get them to at least explore other options and I think that openly I see that as leaning to a better, more civilized adult population 20 years down the road. And I think youthworkers do need to be aware of that and work towards that.

. . . there's some real, real basic ones like, you know and understand a situation which is abusive and you stay out of that. You know and understand boundaries and pay attention to those.

I think youthworkers, if you want to use that term, are people that aren't afraid to ask questions about themselves. I think you can't do good work with a kid if you haven't somehow looked at yourself first and you ask some deep serious questions.

. . . it's pretty boring not to think about those things and not to have that kind of passion about stuff. It's like when I hear kids talk about that, maybe it's sentimental on my part, but I think it would do us all a lot of good to maybe get more passionate about stuff.

I guess the rules would be that they'd begin with caring about youth. Somebody to do this job, you have to have an investment in youth and all the other burn-out and all the other things that come along with understanding that it has to come back to the fact that you care about kids. I think that you have to have the best interest of the youth in mind above and beyond your own interest and needs. I think what I talked about earlier about boundaries and maturity and judgment.

. . . . If It enhances that relationship or the kid's ability or power to choose, then to me it seems like it probably is good or ethical. So, maybe one of the guidelines for it is that most of what you thworkers do is judged ethically by relationship standards as well as how it does from the kid's point of view.

I don't think youthworkers see the world in black and white. It's shades of gray. I think youthworkers are more concerned about the context in which things happen.

I think the task of a youthworker is to help youth discover the ability to choose and the task of a community is to provide kids with choices. I also think on some level, that It's the youthworkers' job to try and get the community to provide those choices. So, it's not just helping, it's sort of 2 pieces to it, 'cause I don't just do the stuff with the kids.

. . . . You never do learn anything from a rule. You may learn something from the person who enforces that or, so just something about relationship and also something about never betraying your client, betraying your kid to the systems that say this is an aggravated assault or a prositute or this or that. Never betray you kid. . . .

115

It's a life; I can say it's a lifestyle. It's the way I look at all – I think it's more of a global approach to what society's problems are. This is something I—what I guess what I do—fits in with my philosophy of life. . . . .

... we need to help other people. The world is basically pretty f – – – ed up and that there are people who get hurt. We need to do something about that. . . .

... somewhere In the admission statement is to develop a relationship. Now what the hell does that mean? What is that relationship? Does that mean that I form a romantic relationship with them? Does that mean I invite them home for Thanksgiving? Does that mean I become good friends with them and sell them my car? What does all that mean, all that relationship stuff? So, I think that's the kind of stuff that I have trouble with. What is a healthy relationship with a kid?

I think that you need to make good decisions for yourself and for the kids that you're with in terms of which way you choose to direct them and things that you tell them and don't tell them but also boundaries in terms of emotion, knowing when you're too far in or when to pull out or when to cut off, when to keep pursuing, that kind of thing. I think that's real important.

I mean there is a certain code there, it's like if I start getting rigid on something, somebody I know that is a youthworker is going to call me on that too. And it's like that's not in the code to be like that.

Well, I think unfortunately because of the big system. I think, the rules that youthworkers live by is how to break rules, because it doesn't work. And I think it comes down to, you got a whole group of people that aren't being treated as people and there's not a damn thing you can do about it. So I think what it is, is that the way you work is to break rules.

... they didn't push it as far as they could push it. Be able to figure out which rule to break, if they, yeah, it would be breaking a rule to just do the easy thing which would be to fit a kid into a system that a kid doesn't belong.

I think there are a lot of rules about respect for the kid and respect for the kid's ability and right to have control over what happens in their life. Which turns into lots of rules about not taking actions on behalf of the kid unless the kid agrees to that. That you do not, and I think this is where youthworkers struggle a lot with other systems and other professions. If you're working with a kid that's a minor, it's the issues that come up when you know that they're going out with or having sex with somebody that is not a minor. You report that as abuse or not, it gets down to nitty gritty issues like that, it's not that you're trying to do what's best for that kid and it won't put that kid at more risk and that has to do with respecting the kid and the right of the kid to be involved in how things happen.

I believe that communication between people should be non-positional. So, the places I've run into hassles or when I deal with institutions or setups or people that believe that there's sort of a hierarchy, that because I'm an adult or because I'm in a position or because of the situation at hand, the adult has control over what the kid does.

Yes, so, I think if I stopped doing what I was doing. right. I would have to forget what I know, and I can't. So, in a sense it's give up who you are?

Who defines it? And who defines, yea, I guess, it's like getting, I think a lot of times youthworkers develop a relationship with kids and I myself have developed relationships with kids that I think in the long term have not been the best, because they have been, it's been more like caretaking rather than being supportive.

It's like I was going to say, I think that's a part of what I'm still developing as a youthworker. I think the limits that I'm still seeing are like inside myself. Like what, I think a lot of times are like boundaries , I don't know if there is ever a curriculum for youthwork, I think that's a big area that is not looked at. It's like, what are the ethical boundaries?

Like, there are people who look at that, what are ethical boundaries for youthwork and your relationship with, usually with, and I think, that's like for myself I'm finding out what that is, I push myself too far, inside. I go over the limits that I'm not comfortable with and that's the kind of stuff that I'm learning about. . . . I think it's more important to see that however each person defines their troubles "is real" to them, even thought it might not be real to me or to you or anybody else and the respect for that realness to them is most important . . . .

. . . I couldn't even tell you what the ethics are or social work and for psychology In a sense, I mean, I know things make sense. That's how I see the ethics is that things make sense and I know inside what's right and what's not right . . . .

I think it's made up of a lot of things. philosophy about the work. I think we mentioned it earlier, I think that there's a value in knowing where young people might step having an understanding of that place that they would step into. My philosophy again is revealed in when I speak of a fondness for young people, that young people do need advocates. My philosophy would have to do, would suggest that I nearly always have the time for a young person. To listen although I may have heard similar stories many, many times. To always listen as, new and fresh as I can. To know that there is a to believe that there is vast potential in each and every young person.

...the jury is still out on who this person is going to be in the long run, no matter what the circumstances have been up to the point that I encounter that youth. In conversations where it's, where the conversation would reflect a collaborative search for answers, for solutions, for understandings. To see youth as every bit as valuable as anybody walking the face of the earth. In the agency we speak in terms of young people as being us only later and I see the young people very much that way. I see them in me.

Yea. Well, they're always on the edge too. I think a good youthworker is pushing that stuff. Is always advocating the rights of youth which I think that's a real important part of the job and again I'm speaking for older, it might be different If you're working in a daycare, you know?

...but to me that's almost a hallmark of a youthworker, is that he doesn't have to be consistent.

And I think sort of this unwritten code says that, no you do have fun. You focus on them, you listen to them. You get an idea of what they're saying. I don't think that's a generally, shared all across the board, though. I think there are a lot of people who work with teenagers, with youth, with kids who keep that sort of professional distance. Don't look at the kid as anything other than a client, somebody you're working with. Don't look at them as a person as much.

Index